The Music of My Life

SERIES ON OHIO HISTORY AND CULTURE

Series on Ohio History and Culture
Kevin Kern, Editor

Titles published since 2016.

For a complete listing of titles published in the series, go to www.uakron.edu/uapress.

The Music of My Life

Finding My Way After My Mother's MS Diagnosis

Steve McClain

The University of Akron Press
Akron, Ohio

ISBN: 978-1-62922-257-8 (paper)
ISBN: 978-1-62922-258-5 (ePDF)
ISBN: 978-1-62922-259-2 (ePub)

A catalog record for this title is available from the Library of Congress.

∞The paper used in this publication meets the minimum requirements of ANSI/NISO z39.48–1992 (Permanence of Paper).

Cover illustration: Rhye Pirie. Cover design by Rhye Pirie and Amy Freels.

The Music of My Life was designed and typeset in Minion with Gimlet display type by Amy Freels and printed on sixty-pound white and bound by Bookmasters of Ashland, Ohio.

Affordable
Learning Initiative
THE UNIVERSITY OF AKRON

Produced in conjunction with the University of Akron Affordable Learning Initiative. More information is available at www.uakron.edu/affordablelearning/

For my wife, Kerri. I can't list the reasons, for they are infinite. There is no one else on this pale blue dot with which I would want to share our brief time.

Contents

Sunset in Franklin, Tennessee. *Photo: Amelie Mendoza*

Preface

What have I done? What the hell have I gotten myself into? Let's pretend for a minute that you and I are in a bar, and we are casually talking. You're buying, by the way.

This book started as a way for me to remember my mom, "Betty" McClain. I wanted people to know that my mom had an incredibly difficult and extraordinary life. I had no idea what I had started or where it would go. I had no writing schedule. I wrote when I felt inspired. Sometimes, that was every day. Other times, I didn't touch it for weeks or months. I am certain that my lack of discipline and work ethic is why it took eight years to get to this point.

I leaned into the "write drunk, edit sober" quote that is misattributed to Hemingway—well, not entirely. There was no small amount of gin and tonic consumed during some of the writing process (or wine, or Scotch...I don't want to leave anyone out). I stuck with coffee while I wrote sitting at a table on the second floor of the Williamson County Public Library with my ear buds listening to chilltronica and ambient music (that's how I roll).

This whole process was cathartic, cleansing, and therapeutic for me. As painful as it was sometimes, I miss the writing process and the time travel I got to experience as I relived so many events and revisited so many people and places. I intentionally left some things out, and I'm sure that I got a lot of it wrong. For any reader who may have been there, you might remember it happening differently, but in my memory, this is how it all went. Who knows? Maybe we're both wrong.

Anyone who knows me knows that I am a musician and that music is incredibly important to me. So much of my life has had a soundtrack. I got my first Beatles record at age five and had a guitar in my hand at age seven. I played my first gig (fifth- and sixth-grade talent show) when I was ten, was in a working rock band at fourteen, and by nineteen, I was employed as a guitar teacher in a local music store. Fast forward to 2019, and I found myself playing guitar on stage at the Ryman Auditorium in Nashville, Tennessee.

The working title of this book was *My Son's Name is Stephen*. This was originally my attempt to give my mother a voice that she didn't necessarily have. But I ended up writing a little more about myself then I ever intended. Stuff that I never considered important was weaving its way into the narrative—gigs that I played, friends that I had, and so many songs. I told a writing friend that I feared I was writing too much about my own experience, and she said, "Maybe this is your story, too." That never occurred to me—maybe it was my story. I continued with that in mind and learned a lot about myself as the project evolved. I shared an early draft with that same writing friend for a first edit and critique. She commented that she felt bad that I had to grow up the way I did. I responded that it was all just normal to me. That was my life, and I never thought much about it. Until now.

Oh, and there is a lot of swearing in this book. Let's have another round...

The first three quarters of my residency on this globe were spent in Northeast Ohio. I was born in Ravenna, lived most of my young life in Newton Falls, bounced around Portage County a little, and would eventually live in Stow for a couple of years. It's a great place to be from, if you know what I mean, but I always wanted to get out. It has nothing

My mom and I dancing, 1986

to do with the place. It's me. No matter where I may have been from, I would have wanted to escape it. Regardless, I miss Ray's Place in Kent. I miss Sam's Pizza in Newton Falls, and, at times, I miss who I was there. But my life has not been there for a very long time. I have lived in Middle Tennessee for fifteen years. That's a long time. I will always be from Northeast Ohio, but now, this is my home. I have a better mental map of the Nashville metro area than I ever did of Akron-Cleveland. I'm sure that has to do with age. I didn't need that map when I was younger. Regardless, I've been here long enough to know this place. Good and bad…but that's everywhere. The winter weather in Ohio sucks, but sometimes the heat here is unbearable. There's a long history of racism in the south; however, some of the biggest racists I ever met were from Ohio. The music in Middle Tennessee is fucking awesome, but Northeast Ohio gave us Devo, Chrissie Hynde, Michael Stanley, a transplanted Joe Walsh, Tracy Chapman, Trent Reznor, Bobby Womack, the Dazz Band, Dave Grohl, Marilyn Manson, Jani Lane, and Phil Keaggy, among others. My blue-collar work ethic comes from my formative years there. I was working and living on my own when I was nineteen. This was before cell phones and the Internet. For those of us in that demographic, we are different. Gen X, represent. Life without the Internet and without being constantly connected was wonderful. You could disappear, and I often did.

This is just beginning for you, but for me, it is the ending. I think back on who and where I was when I started writing. I am a different person in a number of ways. You'll find out later. The sun has set on this project, and I don't know what is next. I do know that I will miss it. I already do. It's been an interesting ride, to say the least. A ride that went places I never imagined. Some were happy places, others, not so much. Either way, it feels like last call.

This one's on me....Cheers.

-1-
Why Me?

Mountain. That was the word she used. I knew exactly what she was talking about, but I am not sure everyone else really got it. A small step. A throw rug. A street curb. The distance from the bed to the bathroom in the middle of the night. When she was baptized as a middle-aged adult at the First Congregational Church in Newton Falls, "Mountain" was the title of the piece of original prose that she shared with the church gathering on that day, explaining what the world was like in her wheelchair. She had to deal with overcoming mountains on a daily basis. I got it. But did I really? If only I had a copy of the piece that she wrote so I could take a peek into her world from the safe distance of a couple of decades. I could look further into her writing and appreciate the creativity and want for expression that she had, which was slowly marginalized and eventually silenced by multiple sclerosis. I had spent a good part of my life helping her overcome mountains. I knew how to deftly spot them, but I could never truly understand her geographies. I could leave it, but it never really left me. Whether others ever noticed it or not, her perspective and view of the world could be seen in the photographs that she took, however unintentional. Any picture that she snapped was from the vantage point of the wheelchair; the photos always angled upward.

I often wondered what night was like for her, alone with nothing but her thoughts: What will I do? What can I do? Who will help me? How will I get by? Why me? Why me. When she heard other people ask that, she would sternly reply, "Why NOT you?" That would shut anyone up. I admired and took for granted her lack of self-pity to the point that when something did get her down, I felt a little bothered and uncomfortable because she just didn't act that way. It left me feeling helpless.

But in her dreams, she danced. That's what she used to tell me. To what, I'm not sure. I can imagine it was to songs from her high school days like "Unchained Melody," "Wooly Bully, "Stop! In the Name of Love," or "This Diamond Ring," well before MS would steal this ability. Either way, when she was in another state of being, unconscious and free, her legs worked, and she danced.

It is easy to forget when looking at someone who has no outward appearance of having a disability (with exception of a wheelchair, walker, or cane) that they have a chronic and progressive illness. "But you look so good" is what people with multiple sclerosis often hear from well-intentioned, but uninformed people—as if someone must look as though they have a disease to be limited or fully consumed by it. I don't believe that anyone can truly understand the effects of this disease without actually having it, but I feel that I came closer than most through my experiences with my mother's MS as it progressed: the uncertainty, the fatigue, the failing eyesight, the difficulty in speaking, along with the loss of mobility, sensation in the extremities, coordination, muscle tone, short-term memory, and fine motor skills. And the flare ups. She would refer to her flare ups as "the bear."

The first major flare up that I can remember was when I was about fifteen or sixteen years old. She was still working at this point—at a bank, I believe. It was a school day, so I got up and got ready as usual. She was still in bed, in her room with the lights off and curtains drawn.

When I came home from school later that afternoon, she was still in bed, lights still off, and curtains still drawn. I remember slowly opening her bedroom door and asking cautiously, "Are you ok?" She mumbled that her MS was acting up, and she just needed to rest. At this age, I was more than just aware of her illness. I knew a lot about it. It had always been a part of my life. But like most teenagers, I didn't know what to do to help, so I left her alone. She would often bring up the time that I asked, with trepidation, if she was "ok" during this particular bout with "the bear." I think it made her feel good that I was concerned and aware that she wasn't doing well, as she smiled and acknowledged "that's just the way it is."

Like most chronic illnesses, this is a disease that does not just affect the patient. It noticeably affects the lives of everyone around the patient, if not directly, then indirectly. As early as I can remember, my mom walked with difficulty and almost always needed assistance. As an adolescent, I would be that assistance whenever I was near. She held my arm as we walked. I retrieved her walker from the backseat of the car. I sometimes carried her upstairs to her bedroom when she was having a bad day. I pushed her wheelchair when she couldn't wheel herself. She needed to park as close to the store as possible and eventually applied for a handicapped parking placard. During family reunions and picnics at my great-aunt Ruth and uncle Deb's farm in rural Northeast Ohio, she was the only one who was allowed to drive her car along the dike back to the lake. Everyone else had to walk, carrying coolers, food, and fishing gear to the kidney-shaped oasis. She eventually got a full-size van with hand controls and a wheelchair lift, which absolutely fascinated Uncle Deb (short for Delbert), who silently marveled at the mechanism as it raised and lowered his niece to and from her transportation.

Not only does this disease affect the people immediately related to those afflicted with it, but multiple sclerosis also impacts our society economically. When she could no longer work due to the fatigue and loss of mobility, my mother began receiving food stamps and other government assistance. To the casual observer, a person who "looks so good" should be able to work in some capacity. She did for as long as she could. Years later, I at times found myself guilty of suggesting, perhaps, that she volunteer to read to children at the library, or something like that, to create some sense of purpose. I could see that an increasingly small zone of interaction and the lack of self-worth was affecting her mental health. These suggestions were met with a laundry list of reasons why not. So I stopped. I didn't know what else to do.

This disease strikes people in the prime of their lives, during the times when they are the most creative and productive. I remember looking at my mother's pencil drawings from high school—self-portraits and sketches of her mother and sister. They were good. I found old science fiction books that were hers when she was young. Why didn't she still have an interest in these later in life? Why didn't she ever pursue art or writing? Why didn't she try to pass her interests on to me? When the majority of your time and energy is spent on surviving and getting through the day, there is rarely enough left over for creative endeavors.

Years ago, I began thinking about what able-bodied people take for granted. How often do we say, "next time?" "The next time we go out, I'll slow dance with you." "The next time we go to the grocery store, I'll let you drive." "The next time I go upstairs, I'll clean the bathroom." "The next time he acts like an asshole, I'm gonna punch him in the throat." What were my mother's last times? Was she even aware that they were the last time? The last time she walked unassisted. The last time she drove a car. The last time she climbed a flight of stairs. The last time she was able to stand to take a shower. The last time she went grocery shopping and prepared her own meal. Simple, mundane tasks that the vast majority of people never really consider. No more. No more independence. No more spontaneity. Nothing more to look forward to.

She was young once. Just like everyone. And like most people, I'm
sure she had dreams and aspirations. I am all but certain those dreams
and aspirations did not include being sidelined by an incurable autoimmune disorder. Who the hell would ever think that? She was of the
generation that was going to change the world. She once told me, "I
had my babies. I did what I wanted to do." But I'm sure there was more.
There had to be so much more she wanted to do with her life that
multiple sclerosis stole from her. I've also wondered whether or not
she would have had children at all if she had known what the future
held. She knew that something was "wrong" late in her adolescence,
and it was hard enough to take care of herself, not only physically but
financially.

I am giving away the ending now. My mom died. She didn't pass
away or enter into the Kingdom of Heaven. She isn't deceased. She isn't
in eternal slumber, and she didn't go home to be with the Lord. She
died. She died way too young. But there is, of course, a whole lot between
here and there. Since she is gone, she can't give me permission to tell
her story. I am telling it as a way of honoring her memory, her life, and
her struggles and to give her the attention that she deserved but didn't
always get. I will do my best not to clean her up in this writing because
living with her was not easy. Watching her die was even harder. My
intention is not only to tell her story, but also tell the story of what it
was like growing up with a parent with a degenerative, incurable disease.
What many people looked at as an extremely unfortunate and difficult
circumstance was just normal to me. I didn't know any different. We
didn't know any different. The experiences of growing up with a parent
with MS affected me in ways that I was somewhat aware of at the time,
but it also shaped me in many ways that I would not come to understand
until much later in life. And as strange as it may sound, I wouldn't
change a thing.

-2-

Rubber Town

My mother was born Elizabeth Ann Pishney on January 10, 1948, in Akron, Ohio. Everyone knew her as "Betty." The time and place of her birth are important. Akron has long been known as the "rubber capital of the world," located in the heart of the industrial belt of the Great Lakes region. This is mostly a working-class population and landscape, not terribly far from the steel industry cities of Youngstown, Pittsburgh, and Cleveland and the auto industry town of Detroit. The whole region is now commonly referred to, both literally and figuratively, as the "Rust Belt" due to the decline and ultimate demise of the steel industry starting in the early 1980s. The jobs went overseas, and the economic impact reverberated from the mills to the machine shops to the bars and the delis. Today, determined wild grass and weeds further separate the crumbling asphalt in the empty mill parking lots. The remnants of the foundries and smelting plants are rusty reminders of what once was an economically booming region. This is a region to leave, unless you like to struggle, but it was at one time a flourishing land of opportunity. You could go to work in the factory straight out of high school, put in your time, and retire well. No degree required. The

My mom on 7th Avenue in Akron

economic pull factor brought many migrants here from the Deep South and Appalachia in the early twentieth century. And to paraphrase Bruce Springsteen as he so prophetically and poetically sang in the song "Youngstown," the smokestacks stretched to the heavens, emitting that beautiful soot and ash that put food on the tables and cars in the garages.

Fifty miles west from Youngstown, State Route 76 cuts through Akron, Ohio. Akron was the headquarters of Firestone, General Tire, Goodrich, and is still the home of Goodyear. The environmental impacts of these industries are seen everywhere. The decayed industrial landscapes and pollution are obvious, but there is another environmental correlation. There are high rates of autoimmune disorders and many different types of cancers recorded in this region. Statistics show high rates of diseases like multiple sclerosis in the Akron-Cleveland area. A study from 2019 reports that nearly one million people are living with MS in the United States, showing the state of Ohio in the Midwest region with roughly 353 cases per 100,000 residents.[1]

When my mother was a child, the family lived on 7th Avenue in Akron, just about a mile from the headquarters of Goodyear Tire and Rubber. The house is long gone, but the prewar brick streets are still intact. She told me stories when I was younger about how my grandma Pishney (her mother) would go outside in the morning and clean tiny balls of rubber and dust off the family car and sweep it off the sidewalk. And the smell. This was long before the EPA regulations that we know today. Even when I was younger, I could never wrap my brain around such a world or an experience, being a child who grew up well after the Clean Air Act in 1955 and the Clean Water Act in 1972. The impetus for the latter was the burning of the Cuyahoga River in Cleveland in 1969. Yes, the river caught fire, and that wasn't the first time or the biggest fire.

This is meant to be the story of me and my mother's life with MS. Since there is sometimes confusion about the disease, I feel it is necessary to directly address some of the medical and technical aspects of multiple sclerosis. As mentioned earlier, there are generally few, if any, visible signs that a person has MS. This is why many people with the disease are asked questions like "what happened?" because of the presence of a cane, crutches, or a wheelchair. People would sometimes ask my mom if she had been in some sort of accident.

MS appears to be a "First World" disease, in that most cases are within the industrialized nations of the northern hemisphere. Just as with real estate, the important factor here is location, location, location.

---

1. "Newly Published NMSS Study Confirms Nearly 1 Million Americans Have MS," *Multiple Sclerosis News Today.* https://multiplesclerosisnewstoday.com/2019/02/15/newly-published-nmss-study-confirms-nearly-1-million-americans-live-with-ms/.

There are more than 400,000 known cases in the United States, but these numbers can only be estimated since the CDC does not require physicians to report new cases. About 2.3 million people live with MS worldwide. However, these cases are not evenly distributed. Multiple sclerosis is much more common in regions north of 40° north latitude and south of 40° south latitude. Accordingly, it is much more common in Canada and the northern United States than it is in the southern US. MS is basically unknown in regions like sub-Saharan Africa or Latin America. It is mostly found in the mid-latitudes and affects those within mid to higher income levels. There are a number of variables to bear in mind when considering why the disease is more prevalent in cooler climates, but researchers have been unable to identify a single contributing factor.[2] The coordinates for Akron, Ohio, are 41° north latitude and 81° west longitude. The city is within the humid-continental climate region where winter is the dominant season. It's cold. It's gloomy. It's industrial. Environmentally and geographically, it has all the common variables.

Multiple sclerosis is an incurable disease of the central nervous system, which is associated with a variety of symptoms and persistent difficulties. There are generally two types of MS, relapsing-remitting and progressive. Most people are initially diagnosed with relapsing-remitting. The relapsing-remitting type is characterized by episodes of recurrent symptoms followed by periods of remission where the symptoms may disappear completely. Progressive multiple sclerosis is just as the name implies. Symptoms continue to worsen over time with no remission.[3]

Most patients are diagnosed when they are between the ages of twenty and forty. A disproportionate number of women are diagnosed in their early twenties as opposed to men, but some people are diagnosed much later in life. About twice as many women are afflicted with MS than men. It is not hereditary, but research shows that there could

2. "Understanding MS," https://www.nationalmssociety.org/What-is-MS/MS-FAQ-s and https://mssociety.ca/library/document/p5eBLiuqo1S4M9Fnz2TYbKQgfmvoajRC/original.pdf.
3. "Types of MS," National MS Society, https://www.nationalmssociety.org/What-is-MS/Types-of-MS.

be an MS gene that may place some people at a higher risk. It is now believed that there may be a genetic component, in that those with a family history may be more likely to develop the disease. The effects and symptoms of multiple sclerosis include everything from tingling and numbness in the fingers to extreme fatigue and muscle weakness. Other symptoms experienced are loss of balance, coordination, and mobility. In addition, others may develop failing vision and cognitive symptoms like short-term memory loss and speech difficulties.

Some research suggests that MS is a virus that enters the system only when one is very young. Seemingly, age plays a very important role in regard to geography. The age at which someone moves to or from countries with cooler climates where multiple sclerosis is more common may be a factor as to whether or not he or she could develop MS. Researchers have found that if a person moves after the age of fifteen years, the risk of getting MS is that of the country of origin, i.e., someone born in Puerto Rico who moved to New York at the age of twenty-one years would be far less likely to develop MS as a twenty-one-year-old New York native.[4]

Some may have heard of the "MS Personality." There is much debate as to whether the MS personality actually exists, but there are definitely some behaviors that my mother exhibited that lined up with what some have referenced to as personality traits and changes associated with the disease. There are many characteristics associated with the MS personality, such as difficulty in making changes, depression, anger, "laughing uncontrollably at things that are only mildly funny" or crying for no apparent reason. Another behavior is saying or blurting out things that should be kept to themselves.[5]

4. Paul O'Connor. *Multiple Sclerosis: The Facts You Need*. Firefly Books, 2005. https://mssociety.ca/library/document/p5eBLiuqo1S4M9Fnz2TYbKQgfmvoajRC/original.pdf.
5. Anne Windemere. "MS Personality: Fact or Fiction." HealthCentral, https://www.healthcentral.com/article/the-ms-personality-fact-or-fiction.

Mom on the farm in Edinburg, 1962

After my mom spent her early childhood in the city of Akron, my grandfather decided to move the family to a farm in rural Portage County, just about twenty miles east. The family had lived close to the Goodyear rubber plant, and he could walk to work at the factory. The air was noxious, and pollution from the factory was everywhere. The farm in Portage County was on land owned by my grandmother's brother. My grandparents (who were never "together" during my life-time), my mom, her sister, and baby brother moved to a faded, white New England one-and-a-half on several acres of land with a barn, granary, and plenty of blackberries. Much of the surrounding land was also in my grandmother's family. Two of her brothers and her sister's farms were within walking distance.

It was 1960. My mom would have been twelve years old. She went to grade school just a few miles down the county road in Edinburg. It sounds quaint, but in reality, it's nothing more than the intersection between State Route 14 and County Road 18 with a feed mill, a grade school that is long torn down, and an old grocery store that always smelled of gamey meat. She graduated from Southeast High School a few years later just a mile down the same county road in the other direction, where she would eventually meet my father. The Beatles hadn't yet landed in America. The Everly Brothers, Elvis Presley, and Chubby Checker were on the radio. She had yet to attend a high school dance, but that would soon change as the innocence of the 1950s gave way to the freedom and liberation of the 1960s. While it was seemingly safer and quieter in the country than the dirty city streets of Akron, far away from the urban crime and the toxicity of the Goodyear plant, life on a farm was hard, and her father was abusive. Going to college was not an option. She only had the limited clerical and home economics skills that were offered to young women in high school at the time. What easier way to escape the farm than to get married.

-3-
Racing

From what I've been told, my parents were the "it" couple in high school. After they were married in 1967, my mother's way of life changed significantly. Even though she was the oldest of three children in a family that struggled to get by on the farm, she still worked as a secretary for General Electric. My father, an only child, worked at the Ravenna Ordnance plant, also known as the "arsenal." His parents had escaped the poverty of rural West Virginia. After living in Louisville, Kentucky, for a short while, they settled in Northeast Ohio. My grandfather had a well-paying job at the Chrysler auto plant in Twinsburg, Ohio. He sold the newlyweds the property next door for one dollar, where they first lived in a singlewide trailer in Paris Township, Portage County, just outside of the town of Newton Falls. I came along in 1969, still proud to be a child of the sixties even though it was the last twenty days of the decade. I vaguely remember my first couple of years of life in the trailer, playing in the snow with Bridget, the brindle boxer, and a first attempt at trick-or-treating that ended with tears streaming down my cheeks before I had even left the driveway with an empty plastic jack-o'-lantern and smeared makeup—I was never really sure what I

Halloween, 1971

was supposed to be. They built a split-level, three-bedroom house in 1972 to accommodate the four-member family, and life was "as it should be." The American dream, indeed. Father went to work in a suit and tie, the kids went to school, and mother stayed home and kept house. Growing up for me was seemingly like every other kid of the 1970s.

At this time, my mother already knew that she had MS. She experienced her first real symptoms when she was about nineteen years old but wouldn't be officially diagnosed until years later. I asked her to write something for me for a speech class when I was an undergraduate at Kent State University. These are her words describing her first symptoms:

> I was nineteen years old when I had my first symptoms, and I had numbness in the tips of my fingers. That progressed into numbness in the backs of my legs and buttocks and then gradually it all went away except for the numbness in my fingertips. That has never gone away. After that, I experienced sporadic numbness in different parts of my body that would come and go and go away slowly

with no loss of mobility. During these periods, at one point about 1973, I went blind in my right eye for a period of three months. My vision came back after that three-month period, and I had no significant episodes until 1975. Between 1967 and '75, I had been through all testing available, which came back negative. They couldn't find anything wrong with me. In 1975, I went blind again in my right eye, at which time the doctor told me I had MS. The prognosis was I would get better, and it could never come back again, I would stay the same, or I would progressively get worse. I really had no thoughts or feeling about my diagnosis when the doctor told me because I had dealt with the problem for so many years that I knew what the diagnosis was. The reason I knew was because I had read and seen different articles and TV programs on the disease and they all fit the symptoms I was having, so it wasn't a shock to me when the doctor told me. My view of the future at that time, I can honestly say, I wasn't concerned about it because I had a family to raise, which kept me busy enough not to dwell on my problems. Little kids take a lot of attention, which takes the attention away from yourself, and I'm not the type of person to worry about my problem. I took one day at a time, and that's the way I do it now. If I can do it, I do it. And if I can't, I wait until tomorrow.

I noticed that there was something "wrong" with her when I was around five or six years old. We had a good-sized garden in the back of our house. I clearly remember walking back from the garden with my mom one summer day. We were nearing the house when I said, "Let's race!" She moved her arms as if to run in slow motion, but she didn't run. She gently bent her knees and (maybe) sped up slightly and "let" me win. I knew better. Even as a little kid.

I also remember us as a family walking through the mall. I was probably between eight and ten years old and just starting to get frustrated with my parents. I was walking way ahead of everyone else, anxious to get wherever we were going or attempting to separate myself from the pack. I have a clear memory of looking back to see my mom holding tightly to my father's arm. It was more than apparent that it was difficult for her to walk. Perhaps it was the agoraphobia-inducing open space of the mall that made it more visible. At home, there are counters, chairs, tables, and walls to grab onto. In the grocery store, there is a shopping buggy. The main drag of a shopping mall is nothing but space.

I don't recall ever being told that my mom had multiple sclerosis or even that she had a disability. I think my father was probably in denial about her disease. I have no memory of him acknowledging it. Maybe he didn't care. After all, he was raised in the generation when "men were men," and I never remember him even picking up his own plate from the table after dinner. Either way, this all was just normal. Her condition did not affect me growing up or prevent her from raising her children. We all tended to our vegetable garden, and I remember her leaning on shovels, hoes, and rakes for support as she used them to turn the soil and weed the rows. We went on vacations to Ontario, South Carolina, and Tennessee. We went on big grocery shopping trips and would spend summer days down at my great-aunt and uncle's lake where the kids fished while she swam and sunbathed. She made all kinds of homemade food and goodies, much of which came out of our garden. I am certain that almost all of my birthday cakes were homemade, along with home-made ketchup, fried mush (a cornmeal loaf that is sliced and fried in melted butter then drizzled with maple syrup—classic Midwestern breakfast), and strawberry crepes on occasional Sunday breakfasts. Many Saturday nights we had homemade pizza made from scratch.

She was a "room mother" at my grade school. Much to my chagrin as a school kid, she was a regular presence when I was in kindergarten and first grade, assisting the teachers, helping kids on and off the bus, and so on. I remember her being there when I was in first grade to give me medicine as I was getting over an illness. She gave me the dose of putrid liquid from a spoon at the water fountain. I swallowed and quickly walked away as she said, "Don't you want a drink?" I held my mouth shut, shook my head "no" and walked away with my back to her, fearful that if any of my first-grade comrades saw me chase my grape-flavored elixir with water, I would be branded a sissy for the rest of my days. That also meant that she went on field trips with the class. I hated it, but I admit that there was a certain kind of comfort knowing that she was there.

She was also the den mother for my Cub Scout troop. The meetings were often held at our house, and she prepared whatever craft or project we as a group were to create in order to earn our scouting badges and pins. During one particular meeting, my father passed through the kitchen and overheard us making fun of the project. He reprimanded me in front of the entire troop because my mother "spent a lot of time and effort" on it. I never forgot that. Parenthood certainly is not for everyone. It's not for me. That's for damn sure. I can't imagine doing everything that she did, and on top of it all, she was dealing with the early stages of MS.

At age seven, I began guitar lessons. It was the same year that I played little league baseball. I played right field, where nothing ever happened, and had the somewhat coveted yet embarrassing jersey number of "1." Even though the Palmyra Hot Stove team took first place in its division, it was by no means due to the stealth and prowess of the team's right fielder, and the guitar ultimately won. I still remember my first lesson at Sound Mover Music in Newton Falls. I still have my first guitar, a ¾ size Crestline acoustic that was purchased there for $25 brand new. I even still have my first pick. And I remain in touch with my first guitar teacher. Though the deal at the beginning was that my father would take the lessons with me, I only remember him attending the first lesson and then half-heartedly "practicing" the lesson with me as he lay on the couch with the TV on. It then became my thing. It was my goal, my joy, my respite, my obsession and inappropriately, at times, my punishment ("Go to your room and practice your guitar!"). It was my mother who drove me to the lessons and made sure that I practiced, though my father, as the breadwinner, provided the $2.50 for the weekly thirty minutes of instruction.

Guitar was what very quickly set me apart. I didn't know of any other kid in the school who played guitar, and that was what I would soon be known for. I have loved music since I discovered the Beatles at age five, along with 8-track tapes of George Harrison's *All Things Must Pass* and Jimi Hendrix's *Smash Hits*, though I didn't really know what I was listening to. I just knew that I liked the sound of the guitars. My guitar teacher's interest in the Beatles only fueled my passion. She eventually gave me her *Beatles Complete Songbook* (because I wore it out. And I still have it).

No one else on either side of my immediate family—cousins, aunts, or uncles—had any musical talent, or desire for that matter, and I loved that it was music that made me different. This was another small connection between my mother and me. She started taking piano lessons a few years after I started guitar. I began teaching myself piano with the knowledge that I had gained from my guitar lessons until it was decided that I needed to learn to play "properly." My sister already took piano lessons from an older lady about a mile down the road on the edge of town, and I soon became a student as well. I learned to read treble clef in my guitar lessons, but this is where I learned to read bass clef. As a young musician who only read treble clef, this was foreign to me (what do you mean that's a C? That's an A!). A new world, indeed. Little did I know it at the time, but my life would be forever changed. My mother began taking lessons also and proved to be a decent player. I was impressed, even then, by how well she picked it up, but even more so now knowing that she had very little feeling in her fingertips. I remember her playing and enjoying a piece called "Chimes" and an easy arrangement of Beethoven's "Für Elise."

My guitar playing quickly evolved, and I formed a three-piece band with two neighborhood friends, one of whom took guitar lessons from the same teacher as me. Our original "drum set" was made out of used, empty, plastic chemical buckets from our pool and a 20" Zildjian cymbal that a neighborhood kid "found" on the road. Pac-Man and Space

Invaders were incredibly popular in the arcades at this time, so I took advantage of his love of video games and offered him ten quarters for it. He bit, but later admitted that he would have given it to me if I had asked. We had a finished basement in the house with an unstocked bar, a loud 1950s Seeburg juke box, and a pool table. It became the band room, and after we scraped up the eight dollars to buy a mismatched three-piece drum set from a kid in the trailer park, it became a concert hall.

We played after school and on the weekends. We played whenever we could until we were told to stop. We had a strobe light that my father and I built from a Radio Shack kit. I found an old color wheel at a garage sale that was originally meant for an aluminum Christmas tree from the 1950s. We strung old-school Christmas lights with the big screw-in bulbs wherever we could hang them, and they would occasionally fall to the floor and melt into the indoor/outdoor carpeting, filling the room with noxious fumes that mixed with the smell of the warm guitar amplifier tubes that was nothing short of sex, drugs, and rock and roll. We played songs like the obligatory "Old Time Rock and Roll," "Turn the Page," and "Heartache Tonight." We butchered "Hotel California" and a deep-cut Bob Seger song called "Long Twin Silver Line," and I played a small Casio keyboard on Don Henley's "Dirty Laundry." By and large, we were ignored and left alone.

But I distinctly remember the one and only time an adult entered the inner sanctum. I looked up from my guitar, and my mom was walking up to us with her clumsy gait. She smiled and said, "You guys are pretty good!"

Before the band really got started, my lesson mate and I played the fifth- and sixth-grade talent show. We played the Beatles' "Back in the USSR" wearing matching red cowboyish button-front shirts. I wanted to play "I Am the Walrus," but my partner insisted that if we sang about that naughty girl, we would both be expelled. My mom bought our wardrobe and made sure that we were dressed properly in Ms. Maiorana's empty classroom before we went on. It felt like being backstage before a sold-out show.

The connection that my mom and I had through music wasn't really a connection that musicians have with one another, though. We could discuss the theory and technique of the piano and take turns playing different pieces from the lesson book, but the difference between us was that she couldn't play without sheet music. I could sit down and pick out John Lennon's "Imagine," "Brave Strangers" by Bob Seger, or Journey's "Open Arms." She would give me a smart-ass look with a squinty-eyed smile and acknowledged that she was a bit jealous of my talent. It made me feel good. She was complimenting me for something that I loved to do. She was really the only one in the family that did.

I was in the inner sanctum, alone, on an early summer evening in July, when I was summoned upstairs to the family room. I was thirteen. They turned off the TV. This was serious. I stood, leaning against the basement door with my guitar still slung around my shoulder.

Expressionless, my father asked, "Would you put the guitar down?"

I responded without thinking. "Do I have to?"

I didn't. The only words that I really remember are, "Your mother and I feel that we can no longer work things out, and we're going to get a divorce." Blunt and cold.

My sister cried. She could do that on cue. It seemed fake.

One of them asked, "Do you have any questions?"

"Can I go back downstairs?"

"Yes."

I went back down, plugged in, and played.

My mom appeared not long after and asked, "Are you OK?"

I kept playing and said, "Yeah. Will you still take me to the carnival?"

My mom drove me to town and dropped me off at the carnival where I had planned to meet my friends. We weren't supposed to tell anybody about the divorce. The first words out of my mouth were, "Guess what? My parents are getting a divorce."

Strangely, I later remembered being in a store in the mall a few years earlier. Out of nowhere my mom asked me, "If your dad and I got a divorce, who would you go with?" Without thinking and with no emotion, I said "you." She pursed her lips, squinted, and said, "I just wondered." Game on.

I was never sure if she asked that out of sincerity or for her own future benefit, but she was the parent who let me be me. The cynic and realist in me both wonder if this was her plan all along because she knew that she would need someone to help take care of her as her MS progressed if she was to ever leave my father. Nevertheless, my decision would be obvious. My father never really liked me, and I don't blame him. I was nothing like him. He was most likely convinced that I would grow up to be some incarnation of Gene Simmons, spitting blood on unsuspecting strangers, setting their children on fire, and giving the family a bad name. She later told me that she knew if they had stayed together that I "would've been gone" well before I ever turned eighteen. She was probably right. My mom let me be a kid and in the back of my mind, I knew that she would need someone to help take care of her. But being a kid was all about to change.

-4-

Fresh Paint

I barely remember moving. You would think that I would have vivid memories of packing all of the possessions acquired over my first thirteen years of life, but I don't. It was an ugly divorce, and my parents would never have a civil relationship like many divorced couples do, mainly because my father had a "my way or the highway" attitude. I represented my mother, and he wanted little to do with me, let alone an amicable relationship with her. He took advantage of my sister's naivete and impressionable youth and convinced her that her mother was a terrible person who didn't care about her. I know this because he tried the same shit on me. This was enough for my sister to choose to go with her father. What kind of a fucked-up court system do we have in this country that allows a ten-year-old kid to decide what parent she wants to go with after a split? There were no parental weekends or court-mandated visits, only a few awkward and stressful meetings that inevitably ended with bitter feelings and unhappiness all around.

My mom promised me $1000 from the divorce settlement money to do with what I wanted, with the understanding that I get a nice acoustic guitar. There were a couple of decent music stores in Warren

My mom working at State Farm Insurance 1987

that had used gear. I bought an old Peavey four-channel PA system with two 4 x 12-inch speaker columns with add-on piezo tweeters from Dusi Music, a Yamaha solid state combo guitar amp with four ten-inch speakers, and a Yamaha FG12 twelve-string acoustic guitar from Bonasera Music. My mom always said it was "her" guitar. The amp and the PA are long gone. I still have the guitar.

It was only a short move geographically, but it seemed like stepping into another person's life. My mother and I moved about two miles east to the town of Newton Falls, a place where I already hung out, but it was a different county, a different school, new friends, and a new place to live. We moved from a split-level, three-bedroom, one-and-a-half-bathroom house with a finished basement, attached garage and in-ground swimming pool to a three-bedroom, two-story duplex that used to be a gas station many years ago. Even though it only had one bathroom, which was upstairs with no shower, it was nice. And I already had a friend in town that lived a block away. Three bedrooms meant that I had one entirely for my music, and at first, I took the larger of the two for my bedroom, but that didn't last long. It was more important to me to have enough space for my band to practice, so I squeezed my double bed into the smaller of the two rooms. The clean and distinct smell of the freshly painted apartment has stuck with me to this day. That smell gives me hope. It was a new beginning. We were both happy, starting new lives. Anything was possible.

We actually moved in the middle of the school year, and I continued to attend eighth grade at my old school illegally while living in another county. My mom drove me to a friend's bus stop every morning, two doors down from our old place, where I got on the bus, and then she went to work. This was a big financial change for us. My mom only had secretarial skills, and most of the jobs that she had were low-paying clerical positions. Maybe she didn't really think it through? I don't know. But I like to think that her desire to get away from my old man was so strong that she would make it work somehow, despite having to work a job while dealing with multiple sclerosis. We also got government assistance: food stamps, free five-pound blocks of orange cheese, and peanut butter with a half-inch of liquid on top, stuff like that. I'm sure that many kids would be embarrassed by this, but I didn't really care. I don't remember the first job that she had, but there were a few: the County Savings Bank, United Truck Parts, State Farm Insurance, the United Way. She tended bar during the day at Steve's L Bar in Newton Falls, a beer joint where guys on third shift drank at 9:00 a.m. For quite some time, she did telemarketing part time in the evenings from home for Farmers Insurance. It drove me crazy. I was a teenager, and it was the 1980s. There were no cell phones or Internet, and she was on our only phone for hours at a time. Hours. Even then, though, I felt bad. No one likes being called by a telemarketer. It's easy to forget that there is another human being on the other end of the line who would rather be doing something else. She was always nice to the people that she called, regardless of how they responded. That's how you play the game. It's all part of the show. As an adult, I have always been polite and patient with telemarketers, though I never buy anything.

After school, I got off the bus at my paternal grandparents' house next door to where I grew up. I then walked the two miles home after hanging with my grandma McClain and smoking cigarettes. She was cool. She knew that I didn't hold the same ideals as her son and that I didn't really fit in with the rest of the family. We were close, and I think she sometimes felt bad for me. Unlike my grandpa McClain who liked classic country music, my grandma liked rock and roll and drank Jim Beam, and I still wonder if her only child may have been an accident. Sometimes I would get a ride home from a passing friend, but more often than not, I walked. I remember it being winter in Northeast Ohio, and it sucked. But it was therapeutic. Two miles in any weather is a lot of thinking.

I spent part of the summer working at a campground cutting grass until I got fired. I called off one day, telling them I was sick. During my shift, the owner saw me on the back of a friend's moped in town. Busted. Summer ended, and I started ninth grade at a new school. Now it was official. A new life. There were several people at school that I already knew from hanging out at the skating rink, the bowling alley, and a few other places in town, but I didn't really know many people at all. This was another big and appealing change. I went from a sprawling single-level school in the country with a forty-five-minute bus ride to a three-story city school built in the 1940s that was straight out of an eighties' movie like *Ferris Bueller's Day Off*, and I walked the three blocks to get there. Life was good. Most of the girls dressed like Madonna and Cyndi Lauper. At my old school, I stood out, but there were lots of people here like me. Unfortunately, no one in my class played

guitar—at least not as well as I did. I had art class second period with
Mr. Sinchak, and he played the local Top 40 station WHOT Hot 100
on the radio. You could count on hearing "Drive" by the Cars and "If
This Is It" by Huey Lewis and the News every goddamn morning. Those
two songs still remind me of those days.

We used to go out for lunch and smoke cigarettes and weed in the
alley across from the school. We called it an alley, but it was really a
gravel parking lot between two buildings. Never mind that the police
station was right next door. Fuck 'em. We did what we wanted. In a
new world where I could be anyone, I couldn't seem to be myself,
mainly because I didn't know who that was. Bad grades and pink deten-
tion slips were badges of honor, and I missed lots of school. I always
felt like I had an image to live up to, being the new kid and all.

Everyone smoked back then. There were cigarette ads in magazines
and newspapers. You could buy them almost anywhere. They were sold
in vending machines like candy bars. It wasn't uncommon for medical
doctors to smoke. My grandma McClain's doctor suggested she switch
to Benson and Hedges 100's because they were healthier. My neighborhood friends and I used to steal her cigarettes. She bought them by the
carton, so she never realized when a pack was missing. I got caught
smoking when I was very young—like seven or eight. My father made
me promise that if I ever started smoking that I tell him rather than
hide it.

A few days after announcing that they were getting a divorce, we
were sitting at the dinner table when my father said, "Go out to the car
and in the glove box is a pack of cigarettes. I've started smoking again
to help me get through this."

I asked, "Can I have one?"

He looked at me, expressionless, "Are you smoking?"

Never forgetting the conversation after getting caught when I was
younger, I sheepishly yet confidently said, "Yeah."

He said, "Well, I told you that if you ever started smoking to be
honest with me, so yes, you can have one."

I retrieved the cigarettes and kept one for myself, concealing it in my sock.

After dinner, my mom drove me to the carnival. She was at the table when I asked for the cigarette. She knew that I had it. Shortly after we left the driveway, she angrily insisted, "Well, go ahead. Smoke! You wanna smoke, light it up! Smoke!" I lit up. It was the most unpleasant, uncomfortable, and awkward cigarette I ever had.

So because of that, I was allowed to smoke in the new place. So were all of my friends. Cigarette smoke was everywhere in those days. Smoking was allowed in the skating rink, the bowling alley, and in Burger Chef. We hotboxed cigarettes in between classes in the boy's room, which was across from the nurse's office in the basement of the high school. Yes, across from the nurse's office. The "band room" in the new apartment quickly took on the permanent smell of a sweaty, smoky locker room with delicate notes of illicitly spilled cheap beer, and the fading essence of perfume and lip gloss. That's right.

We were cool. Seriously. It was the place to be.

I have yet to mention the reason why my parents got divorced. In 1969, the American singer Peggy Lee had a hit with the Leiber and Stoller song "Is That All There Is?" I remember my mom mentioning this song more than once during my adolescence but wasn't familiar with it. The lyrics are mostly spoken and are about how disappointing life can be and how we might as well get out the booze and have a good time—if that's all there is to life. I think the sentiment in the Peggy Lee song may have had a lot to do with some decisions that she made. My mom was having an affair. She knew that her illness was progressing. We all have limited time on this planet, but she statistically had less of it. Definitely less quality time, that's for damn sure. The affair didn't last long after the divorce, and I never met nor saw the man, though I knew who he was. Everybody did. It was a small town.

I don't think that it was ever her intention to divorce my father and continue a relationship with this guy, who also had a wife and two daughters that I would eventually go to high school with. My mom was living fast. She and I partied together a lot. After we moved to town, she went out with several different men, sometimes not coming home until very early in the morning and usually pretty well juiced. I met very few of the guys she dated, and they rarely, if ever, came to our place. There was one guy that she started seeing not long after we moved, faceless to me. I only heard his voice on the phone. She would spend weekend evenings at his place. She gave me his phone number in case of emergency, while I was out with my friends, running the streets and doing what fourteen and fifteen-year-olds did in 1985. The nights away got longer and longer. I remember one particular night, after coming home from being out with my friends. I was convinced that there was someone upstairs. I heard movement. Footsteps. Doors opening and closing. Clinking of empty bottles in the band room. In reality, it was the combination of alcohol, THC, paranoia, and unconsciously, simply wanting my mom home. I called. It wasn't the first time or first night that I did, either. She told me over and over on the phone that everything was fine. I called back. She finally got pissed off and came home. I was still leaning against the kitchen sink when she burst through the front door with her cane and a scowl on her face. It wasn't my intention to lie or trick her in to coming home. Big surprise—there was no one upstairs. I slept peacefully that night knowing that my mom was home, and I wasn't alone.

However, leaving teenagers to their own devices eventually has consequences. One Saturday night, my mom was out with my friend Todd's mother who lived a block away. There were three of us that ran together: Todd a block away and Terry who lived a block to the east. We got into my uncle's homemade apricot wine. It tasted terrible, so we tried adding sugar. That was better. Then we headed uptown. For some reason, I grabbed a rather large chain that was lying around with some other tools on our back porch and put it in my jean jacket pocket. We hung at the bowling alley for a while, and then I left the two of them and headed to the skating rink.

I found out later that after we parted ways, one of them jumped on a car and stole a gas cap in the back alley. They got picked up, drunk, or at least smelling of alcohol. When asked where they got the booze, they revealed that they got it from me. Seriously? Thanks a lot. We were on their radar, regardless. I'll never know who betrayed me because each accused the other, and Terry has been dead now for thirty years.

I was standing in the double doorway of the skating rink when the cruiser pulled up. It wasn't the first time I saw this cop's face. Fucking asshole. I had almost made it.

Some girl walked in and said, "That cop wants to talk to you."

Damn. I reluctantly went out.

"Get in the cruiser; I need to talk to you."

I got in and as he started the car, the cop said, "Some guys at the station want to talk to you."

The son of a bitch tricked me. Luckily, I had thrown the chain I had in my pocket on the roof of the old A&P grocery store before I headed to the rink. There they both were when the officer took me in to the station. Like rats in a cage. Rats, indeed. One went to his grandma's, and the other was picked up by his fuming father. What would I do? My mom wasn't home. I had a choice, spend the night in JJC (the Juvenile Justice Center about twenty minutes away in the city of Warren) or spend a month of Saturdays working at the police station. I chose the latter, but I needed someone to claim me that night. I called my aunt "Marty" (my mom's sister) in Cuyahoga Falls. It was too far, so I called one of my parents' old friends who lived just on the edge of town. They agreed to come get me but soon called back and said that they had had a bit to drink and maybe the cops could drop me off at their house. They did. And after spending about fifteen minutes sitting on the front steps talking with their daughter, I was off on foot. I decided

to risk walking the mile and a half home. When I got to the brightly
lit bridge entering town, I ran like the devil himself was on my heels.
I ducked through the short trail by the water tower, made it home, and
went straight to bed. My mom came home sometime later. Shortly after
hearing her close the front door, the phone rang. She was downstairs
on the phone with Todd's mom, and I heard her say, "I don't know, I'll
ask him."

She yelled up to my room, "Do you know where Todd is?"

"He's at his grandma's."

"Why is he at his grandma's?"

"We kinda got arrested."

"Get down here!"

The next morning, she marched me into the police station to find
out what happened. I can still see the weaselly pornstache face of the
officer on duty in the reversed mirror as we approached the dispatch
window. I spent every Saturday for the next month working at the
police station, cleaning bathrooms, emptying trash cans, buffing floors,
and washing cruisers. It could have been worse. Much worse.

My school days dragged on, and my poor academic performance
inevitably caught up with me. I basically failed eleventh grade and went
to summer school before the start of what was my senior year. Summer
classes were held at the Trumbull County Joint Vocational School in
Champion, a suburb of Warren about fifteen minutes away. I had friends
who also went to summer school, so I caught a ride with them. But
summer classes didn't make up for all of my deficiencies. My mom
insisted—rather, demanded—that I graduate on time. To make this
happen, I would have to attend night school throughout my senior year.
She drove me to class, at least for the first semester, which meant that she
came home from work in Warren, prepared us dinner, drove me to night
class at the Joint Vocational School, (and sometimes) drove home, and
then came back to pick me up after class ended around 9:00 p.m. Then
she got up and went to work the next day. I can't say for sure, but I don't

think my father would have done that for me. In retrospect, I feel like a major deadbeat. This would be exhausting even for an able-bodied person.

I graduated on time. Little did I know that I was supposed to wait after the graduation ceremony so she and my aunt could take my picture. Instead, I caught a ride with an old friend. He fumbled with cassette tapes, trying to find Alice Cooper's "School's Out" to blast through his car stereo speakers as we left the parking lot, but he was unsuccessful. I was glad. Too cliché, anti-climactic, and ultimately sad. Maybe the Peggy Lee song instead? (If that's all there is to high school, then let's break out the booze.) He dropped me off at home and my mom and Aunt Marty soon arrived, where they had a party prepared for me. It wasn't a surprise—wasn't meant to be. The usual suspects were there. My friends, my aunts and uncles, and a keg of beer. No word from my father. I don't recall that he even sent me a card. He had moved to Georgia in 1985 with my sister and his new wife. There were no good-byes, and I rarely had contact. Not to mention that he didn't even invite me to the wedding (or tell me about it for that matter). At this time, my mom had been dating the roommate of the guy who lived next door for about three years. This was the longest and most stable rela-tionship that she had since my parents divorced.

Now that I was out of school, I could work full time. I had never even thought of going to college, and it was never mentioned. To me, that was what other people did. I remember requesting information from GIT—the Guitar Institute of Technology—in California. This was the best guitar school in the 1980s, and many great players in the magazines that I read had gone there. I got the packet of information and told my mom about it. It was $10,000 a year. She said, "Well, I don't know how you're gonna pay for it." So I threw it all away.

I had been working part time at Trumbull Pattern Works in Newton Falls through the school's Occupational Work Experience program for my last two years of high school. The program allowed students to attend school for half of the day and then go to work. I began working there full time after graduation. The shop made wooden molds and patterns that went into foundry furnaces. It was dangerous, especially for a musician, but I grew to like it, and I learned a lot that I continue to use today. I still have the small piece of paper that my boss drew for me so I could learn how an inch is subdivided. Because of that job, I can repair most anything made of wood and have built many things that most people buy, including replacing the carpeted steps in our townhouse with oak stair treads that would have otherwise cost a couple thousand dollars. It was a small shop right in town, and I could walk or ride my bike to work. There were only three or four of us, including my boss, Jim "Buster" Reakes, who had become a friend and somewhat of a father figure to me even though he was only about fifteen years my senior. Eventually, we drank beer, smoked weed, and hiked together. We drank a lot of beer. A lot. I had to work to help out with the bills, and that job was the only way to have any money for myself.

During the summer of my first year of freedom from school, my life was about to change again. I had become best friends with the guy who lived across the street from me. It was a Friday night, and we were sitting at my kitchen table hanging out and drinking beer. My mom was out. Later that evening, she burst through the door yelling that her boyfriend (who no longer lived next door) had been screwing around on her for at least the last year. She went straight upstairs, seething and hurt. I never really liked the guy anyway and, in my half-drunken state, I picked up the wall phone and dialed his number with my heart threatening to escape from my rib cage. I could feel the blood in my fingertips as I told the asshole in no uncertain terms that if he ever showed his face in our home again, I would do him some kind of bodily harm. He never set foot in our place again, even though she continued to see him for a while. Looking back, I am proud and terrified at how brazen I was considering that I wore size 29 x 34 jeans, and he was built like a Cleveland Browns offensive lineman.

So my mom had a nervous breakdown. Her words, not mine. I believe in karma, and at the risk of sounding callous with a "that's what you get" kind of attitude, I felt in the back of mind that this might be payback for what she did to my father. Not that I was happy about it, but that seems to be the way that it goes in the grand scheme of things. Do dumb shit, and dumb shit will come back on you.

She decided to move out. I was nineteen. What the hell was I going to do? I considered a few different options when I told her that I wanted to stay in the apartment. I was working full time and could afford the $285 a month. We met with the landlady, who I don't think ever cared for me or my long hair and convinced her that I had basically been paying the bills for the last year and that my mom was moving because she could no longer navigate the stairs. The landlady studied me with uneasy eyes but eventually, she bought it, and I signed the lease. After that, the breakdown made itself more evident. My mom proceeded to sell most everything. Our living room furniture had come from the formal sitting room in our old house. It was really nice, and I was dumbfounded when she sold it all to a couple who lived up the street for $75. Even they were shocked. She sold my piano. She took the rest of her belongings and moved into a one-bedroom apartment owned by my cousin, Beth, in the city of Kent. She left the washer and dryer because there were no hookups in her new place. I had nothing but my clothes, bedroom furniture, guitars, a gas grill, and the lease on a three-bedroom duplex. The party was just about to start.

-5-
Mobile Meals

My friend's mom from across the street gave me an old green refrigerator that she had on her back porch. When I cooked, I used the gas grill on my front sidewalk. Usually kielbasa with peppers and onions, and an occasional hamburger. I remember being out there late in the evening one night heating up sake on the grill in an aluminum sauce-pan. Strange, I know. I eventually bought a very old stove with wide coil burners for thirty dollars, and I then had, as the bass player in my band put it, "all the modern conveniences." I lived at the deli. Pizza and subs from Continental Carry Out. Big one-foot square slices of pizza for a dollar and a side of antipasto salad. When I could afford it, I got potato salad along with my turkey sub. The place was owned by Frank and Ermenia Guiliano, who were straight off the boat from Italy. Across the street, I dined on pizza from the locally famous Sam's Pizza Shop and also Severino's Pizza and Chicken (and jo jos!) on the other side of town, which is unfortunately long gone.

Since I didn't have any furniture, the living room soon became a rehearsal space for my new band. The new neighbors weren't too thrilled. They were a young couple, just a little older than me. You'd think they

On the cadaver couch in my cool apartment with my Yamaha twelve-string

would want to hang, but they often called the cops on me. We soon rented a room in the old Paris school for rehearsal, and I began keeping house. I got a couple of mismatched chairs from somewhere. One was red, and the other was covered in brown vinyl and didn't have any legs. When you sat in it, you could pretend that you were driving a car. I bought an ugly, out-of-style sofa for $20 at a rummage sale and didn't realize the springs were broken until I got it home. The person sitting in the middle was about six inches lower than the person on the end. A friend gave me an old kitchen table, and I picked up a couple of odd chairs.

I spent a lot of time in Kent. I went to visit my mom at least every Sunday for dinner. It was about a forty-minute drive from Newton Falls. I listened to Stevie Nicks' "The Other Side of the Mirror" and John Cougar's "Nothin' Matters and What If It Did?" (before he escaped the "Cougar" moniker) on the cassette deck in my maroon 1977 Pontiac Grand Prix. Two completely different albums, but they both hit me for different reasons. My car became a cocoon, insulating me from the outside world as the music washed over me.

I started "The Other Side of the Mirror" as soon as I left the driveway. I know the album is loosely based on *Alice in Wonderland*, but it spoke to me. The intro synthesizer and lyrics of "Rooms on Fire" were my companion as I drove down my street and left the monotony of my hometown. The confines of the car combined with the music took me to another place, literally and figuratively. I escaped into a fantasy world in that car and imagined I was somewhere else. This was a solo journey to Kent, but I wasn't alone. I had Stevie and John.

Moving had a number of effects on my mom. She saw the guy from next door a few more times but overall, they were done. She eventually became a bit more mentally stable. Even though the one-level apartment was easier for her to get around in, it was always my opinion that it sped up the decline in her mobility. She lost strength because she no longer had to go upstairs to her bedroom or to the bathroom. The only steps were the ones from the sidewalk to the porch and to the front door. It was one of three apartments in an old house on Prospect Street, just a short distance from Kent State University. She had been alternating between a walker and a cane for some time, but now the walker was becoming more common.

I can't remember how long she had been living there when she told me that the old woman who lived in the apartment behind her had some furniture that she wanted to get rid of for free. It was a big, brown, four-seat couch and an end table. Not bad for free. I borrowed a friend's truck to bring it home. As I was loading it up, the old lady told me with a sigh, "Yeah, I just couldn't keep it around anymore since my husband died on it." Okay. Did not need to know that. No one needed to know that. But I needed a nicer couch that didn't swallow my guests, so I ignored the fact that there had been a corpse on my sofa.

Most every Sunday I was in Kent. We got pizza from Mama Joe's—good stuff until the place burned. I did my grocery shopping while I was there because my yet-to-be-diagnosed panic/anxiety disorder prevented me from shopping in Newton Falls. I was still underage, and there were plenty of places in Kent and nearby Ravenna that would sell me beer, so not only did I drink and drive on the way there, I did all the way home as well. Not too smart, but I was lucky.

I don't think that she regretted moving, but she spent a lot of time back at my place in Newton Falls. There were many people she knew in town, and she was a troublemaker. She wanted to spy on her ex as much as possible in the hopes of finding proof that he was unhappy. I think that this may have been the start of her MS personality making itself known.

The town I grew up in makes people feel old before their time. I was barely twenty-one years old, and I was already thinking so much about my younger days: high school, which I hated, friends that just faded away, old girlfriends, that kinda stuff. Just like walking home during my eighth-grade year, the drive to and from Kent allowed me a lot of time for buzzed contemplation and the John Cougar album, "Nothing Matters and What If It Did," was my soundtrack. I know that the now John Mellencamp doesn't think much of his early work, but that album is now a part of my musical DNA. There are a number of songs on that album that I connected with, but none so much as "To M. G. (Wherever She May Be)."

Just like the character in that song, there were so many things that were reminding me of past events and people. And I was guilty of thinking that those events and relationships were more than what they actually were, just as John sang about putting memories in their proper places, we were really all just friends.

People from my past made themselves present at my bachelor pad, and it felt like it was a constant party. Because it was. I was starting to feel ungrounded, left behind, and for some reason, thinking that the best days were over. So much had changed in a relatively short amount of time that it almost seemed like it didn't happen. We were all getting older. People started settling down, getting married, having kids, or going even further down the rabbit hole. We may have tried to go back, but the good old days were gone forever.

By 1991, I had a pretty good three-piece band together. When I was younger, my band played at the skating rink and a few parties, but this band was starting to get really good, paying gigs. We were playing the more edgy country music of the day and some classic blues rock. Looking back, it was a banal choice, considering we all came up on Black Sabbath, Iron Maiden, Judas Priest, and Mötley Crüe. Maybe we just weren't good enough to play it. We sure as hell couldn't sing it. There are few that have the pipes of Bruce Dickinson or Rob Halford. The music of the day was Nirvana, Alice in Chains, and Pearl Jam. It was a perfect transition to the nineties for those of us hard rockers who didn't fit in during the eighties. It's what we were all listening to, but good luck getting a gig playing modern rock in our little hick town. So we followed the fad of new country. When we did soundcheck at some of our gigs, we played stuff like "War Pigs" and "Man in the Box" prior to our sets of a bunch of Garth Brooks and Hank Williams, Jr. crap. I always felt like an impostor.

Gigs became more plentiful, but we weren't playing for our peers. Much of the crowd was our parents' age, and my mom came to many of the shows. She was hanging out with people that she had known for years, and she would spend the night at my place after the gig. It was fun because the party always came back to my place, but it did cramp my style a little. It's hard to live and act like a gigging rock star when your mom is coming to the show and the after-party. She was either trying to relive her youth or just living it up while she could. Regardless, it was fun, and everyone enjoyed having her around.

It was around this time that she got her first assistant, or "aide," as they were called. I didn't know how to take it or react. There was a part of me that was in denial that my mom needed someone to help her. She was always out to get something simply because it was available, so I wasn't sure if she needed the help or not. This probably comes from growing up poor with very little. Her aide helped with preparing food as well as doing some of her cleaning and grocery shopping. This was also the same time that my mom started receiving Mobile Meals. It is a Northeast Ohio member of the Meals on Wheels Association of America, which assists older adults, children and people with disabilities who may or may not be homebound and cannot prepare their own meals. I have great respect for this organization, but as I recall, much of the food was not so good. And to make it worse, she would often freeze the meals and save them. Quite frequently, she would give me a couple of frozen Mobile Meals to take home, which accumulated in my freezer. Some weren't so bad, but it took many years for my taste buds to recover from the trauma of frozen, thawed, and reheated institutional brussels sprouts. Nasty. Some of the pasta, lasagna, and mystery meat dishes were okay, but I admit that many of them ended up in the trash.

She lived in the apartment on Prospect Street in Kent for a couple of years and then moved to a subsidized apartment on the other side of town. This was a brand-new apartment complex only for the elderly and disabled. It was a much nicer one-bedroom apartment with a laundromat on site—definitely an improvement. I was glad to see her move there. There were no steps, and the apartment was designed to be accessible. Not long after moving in, she started dating a guy who lived in the complex who also had multiple sclerosis. He was younger than her, and I think he was in denial that he had MS. He refused to use a cane or any assistance to walk, and he staggered and stumbled around like Frankenstein's monster. He came with her to one of our Fourth of July picnics at Aunt Ruth and Uncle Deb's lake and almost fell into a table of food. All he needed was a cane. He was a tall, lanky dude with a bushy beard, uncombed hair, and he wore a brass belt buckle that read "You have to lick it to like it." Classy. I never understood what she saw in him. He once told me, "Let's hope they find a cure for this shit before you get it." What the fuck was that supposed to mean? I blew it off. I didn't like him much, and fortunately, their dating didn't last long.

She was still driving the car that she had before my parents divorced. It was a beige, four-door 1979 Oldsmobile Delta 88. Even though I never cared much for cars, I always thought it was cool. It had power windows, power driver's seat, a power sunroof, and a great stereo with an 8-track tape player. This is where I listened to Jimi Hendrix's *Smash Hits*. "Purple Haze," "Foxy Lady," and "Crosstown Traffic" still remind me of that car.

It was around this time that she told me that she was getting hand controls for the car. I think that most people take driving for granted, but it's not a right, it's a privilege. And when that privilege is denied, people in this country lose a major aspect of independence. In most of the US, you need a car. Even in cities where public transportation is readily available, there is freedom in having your own vehicle. As someone with MS loses control and movement of the legs, including reaction time, vehicles equipped with hand controls enable them to continue driving and retain independence. I didn't know what the hand controls would be like, and it honestly concerned me before I understood. My mind went straight to electronics. I imagined buttons on the steering wheel, much like the "accel" and "decel" buttons that are part of the cruise control. How could she effectively and safely use these buttons to drive a car? How could anyone? In reality, the hand controls were a mechanical device that attached to the steering column. There was a lever that stuck out on the left that was connected to two other arms that connected to the brake and gas pedals. When you pushed down on the lever toward the floor, it accelerated. Pushing straight forward toward the dash pushed the brake pedal, and there was a knob, also known as a "speedball" on the steering wheel that enabled her to steer with one hand. The controls took some getting used to. The design also allowed for regular access to the pedals, so anyone could still drive the car. Pretty cool invention.

She continued to have an aide and receive Mobile Meals. Not long after moving, she began using a wheelchair. Again, I was in denial that her illness was progressing. In my mind, I always had the questions, "Why do you need an aide?" Or "Why do you need a wheelchair?" It was also around this time that she purchased a full-size 1989 Chevy conversion van. They transferred the hand controls to the van, and the plan was to have a wheelchair lift installed. She got the lift from a donation from the MS Society and had the lift installed at a place in Mentor, Ohio, which is right on Lake Erie, about an hour north of Kent. She went on her own to get the lift installed. This was a full day for her. For anyone. An hour there, plus however many hours it took waiting for the installation to be done, and then another hour home.

She was excited, but the installation would be met with disappointment. The lift worked fine, but no one thought about door openers. What good is a wheelchair lift if you can't use it alone with no one to open and close the side doors of the van? The guys at the shop tried to rig her something to pull the doors closed with some straps, but it didn't work. She was so let down, but she eventually got the MS Society to install the door openers. There were three toggle switches and a keyhole added in the rear light cover on the side of the van with the lift. The keyhole locked and unlocked the mechanism, one toggle switch opened the doors, one raised and lowered the lift, and the third one closed the doors. There were switches on the lift itself to control all of these, as well. While simple, it was another great feat in engineering.

I turned twenty-one in 1991. A big birthday. It didn't mean a whole lot to me since I had been on my own since I was nineteen. I had been buying alcohol for years, but now I could do it legally. It was a Tuesday, the actual day of the week that I was born. I walked to town in the dark on that cold evening in December to the liquor store to buy my first bottle of legal booze: a fifth of Jim Beam. I grabbed my bottle, walked to the checkout, and the girl working behind the counter rang up my purchase. She didn't even card me. I almost asked her to. It was my birthday, for Christ's sake. I didn't. I just paid for my bottle, left the store, and walked home dejected. I don't think that I even drank any of my birthday bourbon that night.

That Saturday, the keyboard player in my band and I were going to hang at my best friend's place. Wendi and I had been friends since I was about fourteen years old. They say that men and women can't be friends, but we were buds, at least that's the way I remember it. Many people in that town thought that we had dated for years, but we never did. She was living in a trailer park in Lordstown, about fifteen minutes from Newton Falls. As we pulled up to her place, I recognized her boyfriend's car. "I didn't know he was going to be here," I said to my keys player, not that it mattered. I was just curious, since she didn't mention it on the phone. We walked in, and I was met with an explosion of "Surprise!" Several of my close friends and bandmates were there along with my mom. Wendi had orchestrated it all. My first and only surprise birthday party to date. It meant a great deal to me, not only that my friends had thrown me a surprise party, but that my mom had come all the way from Kent, about a forty-five-minute drive, not to mention her getting in and out of her van.

The band was really starting to take off. We were playing good rooms most every weekend in the Youngstown-Warren area and even made our way into western Pennsylvania on occasion. My mom came to a lot of the shows. Many were one-nighters, but we had a few two-nighters at some clubs. Those were always the good gigs. We'd load in and soundcheck on Friday evening, go on stage at 10:00, wrap at 2:00, party 'til dawn, sleep most of the day on Saturday, and play the second show at 10:00 the next night. Those were good times and good money. I'm glad I did it, but I couldn't do it now.

In 1992, I was twenty-two years old. I had been dating this girl from town for a while and things got serious. I don't even remember how we met, but before I knew it, she had moved in with me. The whole relationship only lasted about a year, but at that age, one year can seem like five. We split up. She moved out. I partied. Then I got depressed, and I drank. Hard. I needed a change.

At this time, I had a decent relationship with my old man, even though it was only via telephone. My plan was to take a Greyhound to Georgia. I wanted to stay there for a year to clear my head and then come back to Ohio.

My father said, "Why waste a year? I'll send you a plane ticket."

I didn't see it as "wasting" a year, and I didn't want to fly. I'm a writer. Like many writers greater than me, I wanted the experience of the road. The romance and adventure of the journey is more important than the destination.

"Do you know who rides buses? Derelicts and old people." That's what he told me.

So because I wouldn't do it his way, the deal was off. Like I said before, "My way or the highway." I stayed in Ohio. I drank. A lot. Mostly beer, but boilermakers and Jim Beam and Coke were good friends. And there is nothing like a couple of strong Manhattans at Christmas-time. Or any time, for that matter.

My grandma Pishney was diagnosed with lung cancer in 1993. She was seventy-five years old and already had emphysema. I got a phone call in the middle of the workday at the pattern shop. It was my mom. I said, "Hello?" and in the fashion of the MS personality she blurted out "Grandma has cancer!" and cried. I was at work. What the hell was I supposed to do or say? The cancer had already spread significantly, and my grandmother didn't live much longer. A few months. I had a gig on the day that she died. When I showed up at the venue that night, I told my drummer's wife that my grandma had died, and with wide eyes she asked, "Why are you here?" There was nothing I could do. No disrespect, but the show must go on. I spent that night at my mom's after the gig.

On the day of the funeral, we were leaving the cemetery with everyone else, and the wheelchair lift in the van stuck. This had happened before, and of course, it happened now. It elevated so she could enter the van in her chair, but then it stopped. Frozen. Everyone had gone, and we were still there trying to get it to work. It was like being left behind during a parade. No one there but the tombstones and her freshly buried dead mother. We finally drove the two miles or so back to my grandmother's former house with the doors open and the lift sticking out, doing my best to navigate and avoid mailboxes, trees, and roaming children.

The year went on, and she spent her first Christmas and birthday without her mother. I was still gigging and partying. We played shows almost every weekend and had rehearsals a few times a week. After one particularly rough night, I awoke hung over and sick. I went to the bathroom and stood at the sink, coughing. I thought I was vomiting blood, but I had probably just aggravated some blood vessels in my throat. I was scared. Wendi came over unannounced late in the afternoon with her young daughter to visit. I was still in bed and got up to answer the door.

She told me some time later that her daughter had asked what was wrong with "Uncle Stephen." She explained to her, "I think Uncle Stephen had too much to drink last night." It was April, and it scared me enough that I wouldn't drink again for over a year.

A few months later, I would meet the love of my life.

-6-
Feet First

I felt like life was as good as it was going to get. I was still working the job at the pattern shop that I started in high school. It was a decent job for my lack of education and skills, and it was right in town. I had been there for six years at that point, and I really didn't know any different. The thought of doing something else was daunting, to say the least. So I made a decision. A really stupid fucking decision.

I decided to buy a house with my mother. Looking back, the cynic in me believes that she took advantage of my misguided state of mind to get out of the apartment complex in Kent and move back to Newton Falls with someone to take care of her. The bleeding heart in me believes that she wanted to help me to purchase a house because she honestly thought that it was something that I wanted to do. No matter. It was a bad move, and I should have realized it. I was twenty-three years old, single, no debt at all with a three-bedroom apartment, and the rent hadn't gone up since we moved there in 1983. I could do anything I wanted. What the hell was I thinking? I wasn't. I was trapped within the mentality of that stupid small town. I didn't know what to do with my life, and I needed to do something. So why not buy a house with my mother? Yeah, why not? Because that's dumb. That's why not.

The house in Newton Falls after the wheelchair ramp was installed

I found a three-bedroom post-war house on the other side of town next to the park. Two small bedrooms upstairs and one down with a basement and garage. Still no shower unless you count the creepy, broken-down, plastic stall in the basement. There were more spiders in that shower than there ever were people. There was a bar across the street. I don't know what my plan was. Not only do I question what I was thinking, I don't know what my mom was thinking. The house wasn't even remotely accessible. There were three cement steps up to the small front porch, and she would have to navigate two steps and then the landing to get to the back door. The bathroom had an old claw-foot tub that was tricky even for an able-bodied person to get in to. The place needed some work—new carpeting, a bathroom renovation, and a roof (to be found out later).

Right around that time, I met a girl.

It seemed like the band had become somewhat of a small business, even though we all still had our day jobs. Looking back, we were really just a working, blue-collar band in Northeast Ohio. We had regular gigs in the local bar circuit in the Warren area and just finished our first album at Electro-Sound Studios in Kent, Ohio. (Don't look for the studio. It's long gone.) The album was a collection of my songs that I am still proud of. Well, most of them. The band was very well rehearsed, and we basically recorded everything live in one take, sans vocals. Things were going well. It was August, and we were playing a gig at a big pig roast that was an annual homecoming for the band. I had played there with different bands since about 1988. That's where I met Kerri, even though I had kind of known her already for many years. When I was about fourteen, I got a gig playing lead guitar with a classic rock band with guys much older than me. She was the bass player's daughter. He and I had remained friends for many years. It's a small community and most local musicians know each other. Plus, our families knew each other, and we had attended the same grade school.

Kerri went to college about two and half hours away at Bowling Green State University, and we started a long-distance relationship. In a short amount of time, we were crazy in love. She spent most weekends at my place. This was all around the time that my mom and I were finalizing the purchase of the house.

I remember meeting with the owner at the house, and it was all but certain that we were going to get it. I was sitting in the driver's seat of my mom's van, and as I put it in gear to back out of the driveway, she leaned up from behind me in her wheelchair and grabbed my shoulder the way she did when she was excited about something. I felt sick. I knew this was a bad idea, but I couldn't back out now. I should have, but I didn't want to let her down. I had a history of letting people down, and she had already been disappointed so much in her life. And I thought that she really wanted this.

Overall, I needed a change. I thought that this move was it. In reality, the change was the girl that I was in love with. Now I didn't know what the hell I had gotten myself into.

So we bought the house. I remember reluctantly signing the papers with a knot in my gut. To make it worse, as I signed my name on the papers at the bank, my mom said, "Are you ready for the next thirty years?" which was the length of the loan. Ugh. Really? Looking back, my thoughts are "what was *she* thinking?" I felt that she cared very little as to how this decision would affect my future. What was I supposed to do, work at the pattern shop until I severed some digits on the band saw and live off insurance money? Everything about this felt wrong.

I think the whole situation had to do with control. She couldn't control her disease; she couldn't control much in her life, so she tried to control others. Just like the way that she continued to try and control my father by taking him back to court repeatedly for more alimony. It was something that she could have sovereignty over.

I had fallen into the trap. The spiraling abyss. The inescapable destiny of those that choose to remain in their hometowns. Not that there's anything wrong with that. I wish that it worked for me because there are people and places that I miss, but I always wanted so much more. I always saw myself getting out, hopefully sooner than later.

So we moved in. This wasn't the first time that she said she was leaving a place "feet first," meaning that she was staying here until she died. That's what she said at the last place she moved into, and she would say it again. She had already been living in the house for some time before I moved in. However, since I was only across town, I could move in slowly. We were able to keep my phone number, which was the original number from when we first moved to town in 1983. Everybody knew it. As I gradually moved my stuff, the phone company set up the phone lines so that they temporarily connected to both residences at the same time. This was the first sign that this was a mistake. I had friends, a new girlfriend, and I got business calls regarding the band. I don't know how many times that my phone rang, and by the time I got to it, she was on the line talking to whoever was calling me. Once, when I got a callback from a music publisher in Columbus, my mom answered the phone. This was definitely the MS personality talking—when the publisher asked for me, she said, "He's in the bathroom." Great. Thanks. Real professional.

I eventually moved in and bid farewell to my cool apartment, where I had lived for eleven years. Even though I didn't own it, it was home. A lot happens between the ages of thirteen to twenty-four, and for me, much of it happened there. Sometimes I still miss that place.

Originally there was a big part of my thinking that wanted this because I wanted to help my mom out. Now I had to mow grass, paint rooms, and do small repairs. I wasn't meant for that kind of work. Not that I'm above it; I'm just not good at it. I'm a musician, a writer, and would become a scholar. This whole situation was a case of the idea of something being much more appealing than the reality. The idea went entirely too far. This shit just got real.

Not long after we moved in, we had the bathroom renovated and had a wheelchair ramp installed outside. There was some state or county program that paid for the ramp. She was good at that stuff. Now she could come and go on her own much easier. Even so, the improvements on the bathroom were more aesthetic than accessible. She used one of those plastic, waterproof bath chairs in the tub, and her aide that came in the morning helped her with bathing.

The next year, Kerri transferred to Kent State and moved in, which made our situation even more awkward. Starting from the beginning, I got up in the morning to go to work, and an aide was there. Now there were three of us, with one bathroom, one kitchen, one entrance. The two bedrooms upstairs were mine. One was my actual bedroom, and the other was my music studio. In my old place, I played, wrote, and recorded when I wanted and as loud as I wanted. Now I had to be mindful of hours and volume. When we came in from a night out or after a gig, we had to be as quiet as possible because she was most often sleeping.

Right around that time, I got a great deal on a used Yamaha RY-30 drum machine with a Roland Octapad II MIDI controller that I mounted on an old hi-hat cymbal stand. For the uninitiated, the drum machine is a small electronic component that allows you to program digital drumbeats and the pad controller enables you to actually "play" the drums with sticks. The audio signal goes straight into a recorder or amplifier. My studio room was directly above her bedroom. As soon as I started using the pads to record drum tracks, she complained of the noise. Not so much the actual sound, but the banging from the sticks striking the pads that traveled through the floor. I put down several layers of thick cardboard under the stand, but she still complained. I had some of the coolest gear that I had ever owned, and I couldn't really use it. And on top of that, I was writing some really good songs. I was deflated. What the hell had I done? The Wallflowers were popular, specifically the song "One Headlight." It was winter in Northeast Ohio, and I sang the last verse of the song like it was written for me.

It wasn't all bad. We all had some good times together, dinners, holidays, the Fourth of July with the park in our backyard where they set off the fireworks and have the carnival, but her MS personality and cognitive issues were becoming more prominent. Just about any time I was on my way out, she held me back for at least several minutes with trivial conversations. She did the same thing when I came home from work and when we were heading out for an evening, sometimes for so long that we had to take off our coats because we got too warm. She knew what she was doing. This was about control. Nothing more. I also believe that she saw my girlfriend as a threat. If she could cause friction between us, then there was a possibility that we would break up and she would be more secure. It wasn't the first time that she interfered with someone that I was involved with. This was survival mode.

And she also saw me as an extension of my father (just as he saw me as a representation of my mother). She started taking pleasure in my setbacks, difficulties, and failures. How many times I would hear, "You're just like your father!" It's such a wonder that I'm not more fucked up than I am.

Not too long after we had moved in, I got a call from her at work. I couldn't really understand her. She was so upset and crying. Something had happened while she was at the veterinarian with her cat involving her van—she had backed into the building. Hard. I remember her saying amidst her tears, "I ruined their building!" I jumped on my bicycle and rode the couple of blocks to the vet's office as fast as I could to where she was parked around back. I'm not exactly sure what happened. When she put the van in gear to leave, she slammed into the building, crushing the hazardous waste container attached to the outside wall beside the back door. She didn't actually ruin the building. She was convinced that the floor mat got stuck in the gas pedal causing the hand controls to stick. She angrily threw the mat out into the parking lot, holding back tears. I felt very bad for her because she was so upset and frustrated. The damage to the van and the building was minor, and no one was hurt, though they could have been, since one of the technicians had just walked away from talking with her. My biggest concern was whether or not she should be driving and how to even address that issue.

I had long wanted her to get involved with doing something. Anything. It was difficult for her to read because she had little dexterity in her fingers to turn the pages of a book and the MS made her eyes tire quickly. She watched a lot of TV. Too much. I think much of her television consumption was escapism, just like most people. But it went too far. She sometimes spoke about TV characters and personalities as if she knew them. This house limited her: even though she had the ramp, she couldn't go upstairs, to the basement, or into the garage without help. I don't remember how we managed to afford it, but we bought her an automatic garage door opener for Christmas. She was honestly surprised and grateful and insisted that it was too much money. She had a handyman friend who installed it the following spring. This opened up a whole new world for her, pardon the pun. She began working in the small flower gardens that I had put in along the ramp, weeding and planting flowers while in her powered wheelchair. She was happy, and it seemed to be good physical therapy.

It was right around this time that I started attending college part time at the local branch of Kent State University. I had a few friends who were in college, though most people my age had already graduated. It's something that I had wanted to do for some time; I just didn't know how to go about it. I never could have done it without Kerri's help and support. I walked into the bursar's office and paid for my first course with cash. I started with a summer English class and then took a couple of evening classes in the fall while working full time.

The following academic year, I asked if I could work at the shop part time so I could take some daytime classes. I normally started work at 8:00 a.m. My first class didn't start until 9:20, and my plan was to go to class and then go to work. That lasted about one week. I never felt so awkward being at home in the morning with my mom's aide cooking and doing her laundry. I didn't know what to do with myself. I was much better off going to work for an hour and then heading to class. Overall, life was good as I balanced work, classes, the band, and doing the mundane chores around this house that I thought I wanted.

It was around this time that she "crashed and burned" one night. It was a weekend night, and we were upstairs watching TV. She hollered for help, and we found that she had fallen and was disoriented. Something wasn't right, so we took her to the emergency room. She had been eating lots of deliberately burned popcorn over the last several weeks. Really. We found out later that she was craving it because her sodium levels were low. On the way to the hospital, she kept apologizing, "I'm sorry I ruined your evening." She didn't ruin our evening. I was just glad that we were there. As strange as it sounds, we had a good time in the emergency room. I had flashbacks to my childhood as she stole hospital supplies and stuffed them into her bag. I remember being a little kid in the doctor's office, and before the doctor came into the room, she was behind his desk going through the drawers and looking at his files. I was terrified. Who does that?

Her MS personality was becoming stronger. Either that, or my desire to get out of this situation was growing. The living arrangement was tense. Both of us were in school and my mother continued to try and control me. We decided to move out and found an apartment much closer to the main campus of Kent State. With my classic impeccable timing, I told her on Mother's Day that we were moving out. I told her that I made a mistake. She mouthed, "A big one," and stretched her arms out wide for emphasis. Admittedly, I was thinking of myself (of ourselves), but I did give this a lot of thought. I can only imagine what it felt like for her to have to think about what she would do. Looking back, I don't know that I would do anything different (except maybe tell her on a different day) because the whole situation was a bad move for everyone involved. I felt awful, but we had to do what we had to do.

She originally considered selling and finding another place, but she defiantly decided that she was going to keep the house. It made me feel better, and I was proud of her for doing what she needed to do to get what she wanted. She managed to get the mortgage payment reduced and was able to get discounts on utilities because of her disability. My mother was good at getting stuff paid for. She came from very little and knew how to survive.

We moved about twelve miles or so west to Ravenna, and I still worked at the pattern shop for a while, so I visited most evenings after work. I think that her aides, my aunt, and some of her friends looked down at me for moving out and not doing more to help take care of her. I have said this before, and I will say it several more times: her condition was normal to me. I didn't know any different. I really didn't see our mutual purchase as me helping to take care of her, but I think that some people did. I had already somewhat given up, and now I felt that life was starting over, just like when a movie is near the end, but a whole new plot twist develops. Everything was new once again and I was excited. But I had to balance that with some guilt and the sideways looks that I got from certain people. Now my experiences were growing outside of my little, confining hometown. I was now meeting people outside of the same circle of faces that I had interacted with for the last fifteen years. Sure, I met lots of people at gigs, but meeting people at college was different. I believe that she saw all of my new experiences as a threat.

I unceremoniously quit the pattern shop after nine years and worked landscaping and maintenance at an apartment complex in Ravenna while going to school full time. I still mowed the grass at my mom's house, and she paid me for it. Like ten bucks. I really didn't mind doing it, but I needed the money and gladly took it. I visited and helped her out as much as I could but increasingly, she was calling me to come over and "pick up sticks" and other menial tasks that didn't really need to be done. I know, looking back, that this was just a plea for company or an excuse for me to visit but I had my own life. I was trying to get through school and as an adult; I believed more and more that her situation was the result of many of her own decisions, with exception to the MS.

For better or worse, my relationship with my father had improved. I was breaking away from my band and had started playing solo gigs at coffee houses and small bars in the Akron area, another facet of a new life. It was an exciting, new world. We needed money, and I took about any gig I could get. My father told me about an Irish pub near him in Georgia that hosted acts from all over the country. I sent my father my press kit, and he got me a two-night gig on January 10 and 11. Not only is January 10 my mom's birthday, this one was her fiftieth. Thoughts swirled inside my head. *Do I turn it down? No. Because he would give me shit. Did he book it on her birthday purposely to cause problems, to test me and to jab her? Maybe. Probably. How do I tell my mom that I'll miss her birthday and will be with my father instead?* I could hardly say no to the gig. It was a twelve-hour drive each way, but it would pay our rent for the whole month. *Let's rock and roll.* I was too young to realize the importance of a fiftieth birthday, but I did feel bad that I would be out of town. When my mom lived in Kent, I always brought her a pizza from Newton Falls with candles on it, and she came to expect it. I took her to lunch at Red Lobster a few days before we left. It was a bit awkward. I guess it had a lot to do with this new relationship I had with my father. I don't know. A part of me was still a little kid.

A couple of years later, Kerri and I moved to a duplex a little closer to Newton Falls. I remember having to help my mom attend my graduation ceremony after I finished my bachelor's degree. After she drove to our place, I assisted her getting into our non-accessible vehicle and loaded up her wheelchair. She complained the whole time. I was a bit frustrated that she made no effort to get someone to help her come to my graduation, considering that she recently made arrangements to fly to Georgia to see her daughter with no help from me whatsoever. The only thing she had asked me to do was feed her cat while she was gone. (We made sure to turn on the TV while we were there because the cat had to miss it.)

I really didn't know what to do after graduation. What do you do with only a BA in geography? Exactly. So I applied for graduate school and got accepted without funding. I had nothing else going on except teaching guitar, so we decided we'd make it work somehow. Dave Kaplan, my future thesis advisor, called at the last minute to tell me that the department had found some money and offered me a graduate assistantship. Full tuition waiver and a stipend. I got the official letter, and I remember telling my mom about my options before I made the decision. After some time, she said, "You know that thing you told me about? That offer? You should do that." She had absolutely no idea what graduate school entailed. She barely finished high school, and she liked the eighth grade so much that she did it twice (her words). She only knew that it would keep me around for a few more years.

I started my graduate degree that fall, and it proved to be one of the hardest, yet most rewarding things that I have ever done in my life. I remember telling my mom during my first semester that I had never done anything so difficult, and she asked, "So are you gonna drop out?" She really did not understand. I was working on my master's degree, and she still expected me to come over and "pick up sticks." I know it was a cry for attention, but I was seriously overwhelmed with studies and departmental responsibilities.

She still got around well in her van and even came to our house on occasion. Sometimes unannounced, which was a pleasant surprise. Seriously. We always made a big dinner every Sunday at our place and told her she was welcome any time, just call. She never came once. There were a lot of arguments about how little time I spent at her place, but I made it over when I could. She had an aide that came every day except Sunday, and I honestly wasn't that concerned because overall, she was doing well.

I was still playing in the coffee shops, and many fellow students and professors came to my shows. I was also still playing with some guys from the old days, doing mostly my own stuff plus some cool covers. I met a viola and keyboard player during my time teaching at Cuyahoga Falls School of Music in Stow. Matt and I are still friends to this day though we are half a country apart. We did countless duo shows in the coffee houses and bars at places like Borders Books and Music, the Riverfront Coffee Mill, and the Old Whedon Grille (all gone now), along with band gigs like the Cleveland Music Festival, the Hard Rock Café, and Rockin' on the River in Cuyahoga Falls.

Then to make my life more stressful, I decided to record an album during grad school. A word of advice: don't do that. I had a bunch of new original songs and some other older stuff that we all reworked that my band had been playing live. This would be my second project to be recorded at Miles Robert Audio in Cuyahoga Falls. The studio had a great live room, and that's pretty much how we recorded—live—vocals and all. Looking back, I never should have done it. The recording and production were great, but I was seduced by a distribution opportunity. A paid music service, which shall remain unnamed, was offering a possible chance at distribution through Borders Books and Music nationwide. Submissions would be judged on audio and production quality, songwriting, and packaging. The songs were done, but we rushed the recording to meet the deadline. I was convinced that I couldn't get the same emotive feel vocally doing overdubs, so we kept the scratch vocals. The mixing was rushed. On the other hand, the physical product was great. Guess what? I didn't get forwarded for consideration. We pressed one thousand CDs, which cost me a lot of money. I gave more away and threw more out than I ever sold. I still think some of the songs are good, but I don't listen to that album, and I don't want anyone else to either.

Then we got a call late one night. My mom was getting up to use the portable toilet in her bedroom and fell between the nightstand and her bed. She was stuck, and fortunately the phone was on the nightstand. When you only have upper body strength, you are dependent on your arms to transfer from bed to chair. One false move and down you go. She used to say, "The floor came up and hit me." We drove the seven miles over, got her up and back in bed. Nothing broken, but it could have been much worse. Looking back, I should have done a lot of things.

-7-

You Can't Stay Here

There is a senior living apartment building on the other side of town, right across the street from the West Newton Falls Cemetery. There's a joke to be made here, but it's too easy. She had been on the waiting list to get an apartment for some time. I was a little surprised and quite a bit relieved when she told me that she was moving there. She didn't meet the age requirement but was able to get an apartment because of her disability. Once again, she said she was leaving here "feet first." I was doing music full time, gigging, and teaching at Music for Kids in Stow, just outside of Akron. It's a tough way to make a living. I was busy, but I was able to help her move during the day.

The apartment was small: one bedroom, one bath, a living room, and galley-like kitchen as you walked in the door. She was on the first floor, apartment 111, just a few steps from the common area. I hated for her to leave the house that she had worked so hard to keep and make her own, but it just didn't make sense for her to stay there. Moving to this small apartment was such a drastic change, but I knew that it was a good thing. Nevertheless, I shouldn't have spoken so quickly and should have chosen different words when she asked me, "So, what do you think?" I looked down at the carrot-orange Formica countertop that extended from the wall that also served as a kitchen table while the institutional smell invaded my sinuses and I said, "I don't think much of it," thinking of her living there compared to the house. She turned away from me in her wheelchair and said, "Well, you don't have to live here." I immediately felt like a dick. Still do. Later, as I helped her move in, she was leaning over in her chair attempting to put plastic bowls and containers away in a lower kitchen cabinet, and she broke down crying. I'm not a "huggy, touchy" person, but I instinctively reached out and touched her shoulder and said, "It'll be ok."

Scott Russell Sanders wrote in *Staying Put*, "Merely change houses and you will be disoriented; change homes and you bleed." She was doing both, changing houses and homes. She had a small amount of independence in the house, but the senior living apartment building had its own culture. However, I don't think that either one of us really had a "home" anymore. The specific places where our respective child-hoods took place were gone forever.

Not long after she was settled into her new apartment, I made another move. My girlfriend was now my wife, and we both had finished our master's degrees. We were the first in both of our families to do so. We had been traveling a bit and had the opportunity and desire to move to a small town just outside of Nashville, Tennessee. We had nothing to lose, though I did feel a bit guilty about leaving. We decided that giving it one year was no big deal, even though it was a big move geographically.

I consulted with my friend Mike Talanca, owner of Tune Town recording studio in Newton Falls. He was the real deal. No one would ever guess that this gem of a world-class studio was in downtown Newton Falls, Ohio, a backwater town of roughly five thousand people. He had spent about five years in New York City where he was the chief technician at Right Track Recording, working with artists like David Bowie, Bruce Springsteen, and Mick Jagger before opening his own studio in New York's SoHo district. He got credit on Foreigner's "Inside Information" and David Bowie's "Tin Machine" albums. I remember first meeting with him when I was about nineteen years old, right after my mom moved to Kent. He came over to my place by request of a mutual friend and told me "If you want to make it in the music industry, you've got to be in one of the major music hubs; New York, Los Angeles, or Nashville." Since then, he had mixed one of my albums that was recorded in Kent.

I never forgot that first meeting, and I talked with him at his studio about this decision. He asked me, "What's the worst that can happen?" I said, "Nothing." He replied, "Nothing," with his adopted Jimmy Iovine-like New York attitude. "You can play in Northeast Ohio for the rest of your life, and nothing is going to happen. Give it a year, and if it doesn't work out, come back." I later sent him a Nashville post card and wrote, "Thanks for the right words at the right time."

My insides were tingling with excitement. I went straight from the studio to my mom's apartment to tell her the news. She was sad and disappointed, but I remember her saying, "You've got to live your life. There's nothing for you around here." She never really held me back, but I did get the feeling sometimes that she wanted me around, even though she never said it. I honestly don't know what I would have done if she had said that she wanted me to stay.

So we moved to Franklin, Tennessee, a suburb of Nashville just about twenty miles south of the city. We knew no one there, and many people who knew us in Ohio were puzzled by this bold move. We had visited the area the year before for a conference, and we were attracted to the city, the weather, and the music. Kerri got a job in the public schools within her field of speech-language pathology, and I taught as an adjunct instructor at a branch of Columbia State Community College. It was tough. The schools paid much less than in Ohio, and the pay rate for part-time instructors at the community college was paltry. I had come from one of the best geography programs in the country, and the resources of the community college were eye-opening to say the least. To supplement my adjunct income, I eventually got a job managing a small music store in nearby Spring Hill.

It was at the music store that I got the call from my mother that she had to put her cat down. His name was C. B., which stood for Cry Baby because he meowed so much as a kitten. She got him in 1984 from the brute of a guy that she dated from next door that I threatened with bodily harm after he cheated on her. We weren't allowed to have pets in that first apartment, but she ignored that rule, mainly because she argued that I had done more damage to the place than a cat ever could. She was right. She had quite a past with that cat. As a kitten, he would run down the steps in the morning in front of her and without being able to stop, rammed his head into the wall at the bottom of the staircase. The cat would not come into my room when I was around, but I would occasionally wake up on weekend mornings in the summer to find him lying in the sill of the east-facing open window in my room to enjoy the air coming through the screen. I will never forget waking up one morning to find the screen pushed out of the window. The cat was gone. We found him sitting on the ledge outside of the kitchen window crying to be let back in. I can only imagine how funny it must have been to be driving by and see an orange cat plummeting from a second story window to the concrete sidewalk below. They always land on their feet, right? I guess he did. She had C. B. for nineteen years. Now he was gone.

Most of our time in Tennessee was dark. We were struggling to get by on very little. We had a one-bedroom upstairs apartment with no room for much of anything. It was a cool little place, and if nothing else, it was a great reason to purge a bunch of unnecessary junk. I certainly had no delusions of grandeur, but one of the reasons I came to Nashville was for music, and I wasn't having much luck. Nashville is a wake-up call for many people who have aspirations in the music industry. Even if you are the biggest fish in your hometown, you are average there, at best. These are some of the best players and songwriters in the world. Even so, I got a song played on a popular local radio station and got my name mentioned in an article in *The Tennessean* newspaper for a performance after just a few months of being there. We made frequent trips back to Ohio for gigs and visits, and I had a feature story printed in the *Warren Tribune* after I released my new CD. They are always interested in people who do something outside of the area. I listened to the Vanderbilt University student radio station a lot. I am sure that student DJs don't think that their time on air is important, but some of them changed my life (shout out to the DJ with the show called "I Like Songs"). The music was my escape and companion. On that station, I discovered acts like Death Cab for Cutie, Butterfly Boucher, and the song "Homesick" by Kings of Convenience. That song hit me. Hard. The lyrics sounded like they were written for me. I certainly didn't know what I was doing there, and I no longer knew where "home" was.

We gave it our best shot, but in a year's time, we were already making plans to move back to Ohio. It just wasn't working. Kerri was offered a really good job at Kent City Schools for considerably more money. I was welcomed back with open arms to my music teaching gig. I was hired as an adjunct instructor at The University of Akron for a lot more money than the community college in Tennessee. It just made sense. There is a part of me that wishes we had stayed because, for better or worse, I know I would be a different person today. Judging by her smirk that she did little to conceal, my mom was snidely happy that we were coming back, but I felt like a failure.

While looking for housing, my mom's MS personality made itself even more present, or maybe it was just another aspect of her controlling me. We were coming in for a weekend to sign the lease on an apartment, and she asked, "Where are you staying? You can stay here if you want. I have a pullout couch." I had never even considered that. We had a dog and besides, she only had one bedroom. But we were both more than a little homesick, and it kind of sounded like fun. Like camping. So we said what the hell. We were in Ohio and had just left the apartment complex after signing the lease and were heading to her place when my cell phone rang. "You can't stay here. The dog's not allowed," my mom said with a smug tone to her voice. Jesus pole-vaulting Christ, she had two fucking weeks to make sure that this was all okay, and I'm getting this call now? Fuck. As if all of this wasn't stressful enough. We managed to stay at my father-in-law's place. I was livid.

We went over for a short visit before heading back to Tennessee, and she said, "Well, good. Now that you're coming back, you can help me look for a dog." I said, "You're probably not gonna see too much of me." She paused and said, "Well never mind then." I just wanted the hell out of there, and when we did make the move back, I didn't visit that often.

We spent two years at a nice apartment complex in Stow, Ohio, just outside of Akron. I could walk or ride my bike to my music teaching job and within a year I was teaching as an adjunct geography instructor at both The University of Akron and Kent State University. I worked half days, basically 8:00 a.m. to 8:00 p.m. I had three courses at Akron and two at Kent, then I taught guitar until 8:00 p.m. Monday through Thursday. At the time, most full-time, tenured professors taught only two or three courses a semester. I taught five classes, and I had about thirty-five guitar students on top of it. We were crazy busy, but life was good. We went out for dinner and drinks several times a week in downtown Kent, and I was playing with some great musicians that I had recently met. I miss those days. There are some records that I have to listen to from beginning to end, and Coldplay's X&Y is one of them, back when albums mattered. More than once, I remember sitting on our balcony at the apartment with headphones and a bottle of Chardonnay. I shut my eyes with my glass of chilled Chard and let the lyrics of "Square One" sink deep into my subconscious. I knew that things were going well for us, but at times, I was still restless. I still felt like I was stuck in square one.

I didn't spend that much time in Newton Falls. It's about a forty-five-minute drive, and my life was not there. It hadn't been for a long time. We would visit most weekends, but not always. Her condition was fairly static. She hadn't had a big flare up for a long time, and she was giving herself injections of Copaxone every day, which is an effective drug in preventing relapses in MS patients. One of the side effects is destruction of the tissue under the injection site. The outside of her left bicep was starting to look bad—almost as if pockets of the fat and tissue had simply been removed. It doesn't come back. Considering everything, her health was pretty good, but she was slowly giving in to many challenges. She didn't go out much. She really didn't need to since her aide did her grocery shopping, plus she continued to receive Mobile Meals. I think the only time she went out was for doctor's appointments. She socialized with the old women (or, as I called them, the "old hens") who met in the common area at the same time each day. I always felt like they were giving me looks every time I came around, which admittedly was not often. It was personal.

First off, it was uncomfortable because she didn't seem to have much interest in what I was doing or what I had to say and, at the risk of sounding pompous, we had grown apart intellectually. I was also put off because she didn't really acknowledge that having to move back to Ohio hurt me. Like many people with multiple sclerosis, her zone of interaction was incredibly small. One of the exercises that I will sometimes give to my geography students is to create a map of their zone of interaction by recording all the trips they take over the course of a couple weeks or a month. Zones of interaction vary regarding age, interest, and mobility. There is a correlation between youth and large zones of interaction and elderly or disabled people and small zones. We traveled when we could. I interacted with students and faculty at two different major universities, had relationships with music students and their parents, went to shows, performed music all over the region, and met friends and colleagues socially on a regular basis. In contrast, she rarely left her small apartment and saw the same people almost every day. We no longer had much in common.

I am sure that the outsider looked at me as a selfish son who didn't care about his disabled mother. They could never understand how much her disability was normal to me. I knew what she could and couldn't do, when she needed help, and how to provide it. I also knew that she wouldn't listen. She just seemed spiteful, and I resented it. Maybe it was the MS, but it was becoming increasingly difficult to interact with her. As with many MS patients, her life involved a routine, which is comforting and reliable, but her routines made it very difficult to have a normal relationship with her. Her aide was there between 8:00 a.m. and noon. She napped between 1:00 and 4:00 p.m. and saw no visitors. She ate dinner around 4:30 or 5:00 and was in bed by 7:00. When I visited, I usually had a couple of beers before, during, and after.

In 2008, my mom turned sixty. Probably a year before, I remember her saying that she wanted a party. I certainly wasn't against it, but I don't know who I would have invited. She had alienated most everyone that she had been close to. She had dated many guys over the years who were willing to take care of her, but she always split up with them for petty reasons, or she pissed them off with unrealistic expectations. And she would never even consider a marriage proposal because that would mean she could no longer get alimony from my father. Her visits with the "old hens" were all but over because there were a few of them that she was at odds with. She rarely saw her brother. She hadn't spoken to her sister in years over something that didn't even happen. I felt that she treated me with contempt. As my great-uncle Howard later commented, she had nothing but time. Time to sit and think. Progressively, thoughts or fears became reality to her.

So I planned her birthday. I special-ordered a cake from the Acme grocery store bakery where I lived. (Not to be confused with the Acme company that makes the anvils and explosives for Bugs Bunny cartoons.) It was German chocolate and decorated very nicely with "Happy Birthday Mom" written in pale pastel against the chocolate icing. I came over around noon and bought lunch as well. And I gave her a weird card. That's what I do. We spent the afternoon together and had a really good time. I know she enjoyed it because I knew her. As I was leaving later in the afternoon to go teach, I leaned down and hugged her and said, "Happy Birthday." She looked around nodding her head and said, "This was nice." That's also what she did after a good Christmas Day or Thanksgiving. I knew she meant it, and it made me feel good.

It was clear that she was getting tired of fighting. Even before she turned sixty, she had stopped dressing for the day. At least not like she used to. She had always taken pride in her appearance, and this change disturbed me. Not that she was dirty or unkempt, but she was doing as little as possible regarding her clothes, makeup, and hair. In my eyes, she had always been so strong, and this was hard for me to handle, though I never expressed it. I think she was giving up, and I was about to deal her another blow.

Things were going well for us in the Akron area. We had just moved to a nice two-bedroom townhouse with a full basement. I could record and have rehearsals in the basement, there was a great pizza joint just around the corner, and Ray's Place in downtown Kent was only ten minutes away. If we were to ever buy a house, this place was ideal for us. But we were restless, and a part of us was still in Nashville. Or just somewhere else. I had been toying with the idea of starting my PhD since I finished my master's but wasn't really sure. Kerri had been offered a clinical therapy position in Nashville. She had already turned the job down twice, and I didn't want her to miss this opportunity. It's one thing to have Kent City Schools on your resume and a whole other thing to list a clinical therapy position at a major university hospital. Once again, it was time for a change.

We were at my mom's place for a weekend visit when we decided to tell we were going back to Nashville. I said to my wife, "Well, do you want to tell her?"

My mom's eyes widened, she half smiled and said, "You're not!" She thought Kerri was pregnant.

She said, "I got a new job."

"Oh. Ok. Where?"

"Nashville," I said.

My mom's expression changed immediately as she uttered, "Oh."

She was heartbroken. I could tell. We told her we were moving in two weeks. It all happened very fast. Looking back, I can't believe that we did what we did. We hadn't even been in our new place a year and we packed our belongings into a PODS shipping container and moved into a townhouse five hundred miles away in Franklin, Tennessee. We had never even set foot in the new townhouse. Pretty crazy. We left in a flurry, and I told her we would see her in a couple months. I know she was sad, and she probably felt abandoned and alone. I was in denial as to her condition. Her health and her mental state were declining.

-8-

Jack and Back

We were back in two months for a long weekend. I wasn't really prepared for what I would witness when we came to visit. There was a part of me that didn't see my mother changing, much like she still saw me as a longhaired kid in high school who would never fly in a plane, wear dress clothes, or get married. We don't want our parents to change. We expect them to always be there for us, and when they start to age and are in failing health it is a reminder, if only subconsciously, that we are all aging, and our lives will never be what they once were. Her bedroom was beginning to resemble a hospital room with bottles of medicine, boxes of tissue, an institutional water pitcher, oral thermometer, extra linens, absorbent pads, a portable toilet, and a bed trapeze to help transfer her to her wheelchair. She had the trapeze when she lived in the house across town but didn't really use it. Her aide buzzed us into the building. When we entered the apartment, my mom was lying in her bed wearing her night gown and flossing her teeth, almost as if she was putting on a show so we knew how bad her condition was. She was good at making people feel guilty, but I don't think that this was an act, entirely. She didn't say much and didn't really seem glad to

Me with my vintage Peugeot road bike

see us. I felt terribly uncomfortable. I didn't know what to do with myself or with her. We awkwardly sat on kitchen chairs that we brought into her bedroom and attempted to have a conversation. I poured myself a shot from the bottle of Jim Beam that I knew she kept in her cupboard. I don't remember much else about that visit, and not because of the bourbon.

So after a couple of days, we headed home to Tennessee with the intention to be back for the holidays. I had an interview for a full-time faculty position at one of the larger universities in Middle Tennessee. I felt confident. After my time at Kent State and The University of Akron, my teaching experience was significant, and the interviewing committee led me to believe that the position was mine during the interview process. Life lesson learned. Fortunately, we weren't dependent upon it. I got the call that the job was offered to another applicant. I was truly shocked. I called my mom to let her know that I didn't get the gig, and with a concerned tone, she asked, "So what are you going to do?" I snapped back, "I don't know!" partially because of my frustration and partially because I really didn't have an answer. What *was* I going to do? Those were dark days, not only because of my own shortcomings, but also because every time I talked to my mother, her condition was declining, and it was more difficult to understand what she was saying. The MS and medications were affecting her speech.

There were a few other things that didn't work out the way that we hoped, and given the choice, I think we would have headed back to Ohio. Life was good for us there, and it made us question our decision to relocate. Again. I was depressed and writing songs like mad as a means of releasing my frustrations. Many of these songs would end up on my next album. My favorite and most relevant to me at the time was probably "Not So Good Old Days."

> Is it too early to start drinking?
> 'Cause I've got nothing better to do
> I spent the whole day thinking
> And I still don't have a clue
> It's been too long since I felt like
> I did so long ago
> Every day I get further away
> From the place that I wanted to go

She had several different aides during these times. They either quit or she fired them, sometimes for no reason other than that she was looking for conflict. She lived on a very fixed income from alimony and Social Security and also received food stamps and the Mobile Meals. I was in regular contact with her and was hoping for some kind of parental guidance because I really didn't know what I was going to do. I regretted a lot regarding our relocation. She was still my parent, and I wanted her to "fix" it, but those days had long passed. Now she needed fixing. I remember telling her once on the phone that I was just "tired of things not working out." She said, "Tell me about it." That shut me up.

> But I know somewhere in time
> The words will finally rhyme
> And then I will be on my way
> Away from these not so good old days

Many people with MS have trouble with urinary and bowel control. They may not know that they have to go until it is too late because those nerves aren't working properly. Urinary problems are the most common. My mom experienced many urinary tract and bladder infections because her bladder didn't always empty completely. She kept a large coffee can in her van that she often used when traveling even a short distance. Like many other people with MS, she would push on her bladder to "see if she had to go" before leaving the house or beginning a meal. She had used catheters for a long time to better empty her bladder (which also contributed to infections) until it finally became too much. She opted to undergo a suprapubic cystostomy, which is also known as a suprapubic catheter. After the procedure, there is a hole or a "port" in the lower belly that drains urine into a bag. This surgery is routine and common among people with spinal cord injuries and other conditions where it is not possible for them to empty their bladder completely on their own. She was happy to get it and willing to undergo the surgery because it meant that she would no longer have to risk traveling to the bathroom at night or urgently rushing to the toilet at other times. Unconsciously, I felt it was another part of her that was giving up. Not that I saw her as weak or to be judgmental, rather, I didn't want her to stop fighting.

I don't recall the name of the last aide that she had, but she and I had many conversations. Let's call her Barb. Barb truly cared about my mom's well-being and called me numerous times after leaving her apartment to convey that she did not know what to do. My mother was getting increasingly difficult to deal with. Also, over the last several years, some of the meds that she took made her mouth very dry and it was hard to understand her on the phone. To make it worse, she wouldn't hold the phone near her mouth, so it was also hard to hear her. She had recently gone to the Cleveland Clinic for an appointment with specialists to evaluate her condition. They told her that there was nothing they could do. She had been on current drug therapies such as Copaxone and Avonex, but because of the time of her diagnosis, the disease had progressed so much that these therapies were ineffective. I called her after her visit to the Cleveland Clinic and she told me that "they don't know what they're talking about." I said, "okay."

Barb called me on a regular basis, and she was concerned about elder abuse because my mom needed more care than an aide could provide. I felt helpless. I was five hundred miles away, and even if I was there, there was still nothing I could do. I didn't own a home, and I didn't have any money. There are plenty of people out there who are able to support their aging and ailing parents. Not me. I can barely take care of myself.

It was a surprise to everyone involved when my mother told Barb that she could leave her key on the table before she left at the end of the day. She was fired. We'll never know why. She was one of the best aides she had ever had. Regardless, a few days later, it was a shock and a relief when I called and Aunt Marty, my mom's only sister, answered the phone.

I cannot describe the feeling that I had the day when I called and asked for my mom, and the voice on the other end said, "Hi Stephen! It's your aunt, Marty. I've been taking care of your mom." I hadn't talked with her in several years, mainly because my mother hadn't talked to her in several years either. There had been so many times that I wanted to call her because I didn't know what to do, and I felt that I needed to do something. But I didn't. Now she was on the other end of the phone, and I felt a bit like a little kid who had just gone to bed with both parents home and the covers up to my chin with a fire burning on a cold winter's night. Safe. "I've been helping take care of her for the last few weeks," she said as I attempted to conceal the relief in my voice. We talked for a bit, and she explained some details regarding her aides and the care that she was providing.

Later, she called from home and told me the rest of the story. My mom had called her out of the blue one day after not speaking for years and gave her all kinds of hell. Then she asked if she would come take care of her. She knew that she needed more help than her aides could provide. My aunt couldn't say no to anyone. She had taken her own mother in to her home when she was in the last stages of cancer, and she died in her house. She took care of her ailing father in his last days. She would not say no to her only sister, and this is why I wished that I had called her years ago. Now I didn't have to.

My cousin, Beth Ann (named after my mom) had purchased Aunt Ruth and Uncle Deb's home and farm with the lake where we used to have family reunions and the Fourth of July picnics. She had a modular home built on a small portion of the property, where Aunt Marty (Beth's mother) had been living for the last several years. Even though it was only about fifteen miles away, my mom and her sister had not had any contact. My aunt had now been my mother's primary care giver for several weeks. One day she called to tell me that my mom was going to move in with her. Once again, I was surprised and relieved. My mom did not need to be living alone and needed much more care than the aides could provide. She needed someone around the clock, and short of moving in to assisted living, this was her only option, especially after her daughter offered to move her to her home in Georgia and then changed her mind.

The next time I talked to my mom, she said, "so what do you think of my move?" I said, "I think it's great," which was true. The fact that she was basically trapped in her apartment ate at me both consciously and subconsciously. In my aunt's house, she would have a large master bedroom with an attached bathroom, which was more of a convenience for her caregivers because she rarely left her bed. Every couple of days, a nurse visited to do what my mom called her "bowel routine." You figure it out. There were two other bedrooms in the house for my aunt and her husband, Guy. (He is her second husband, and I don't know why I've never called him my uncle. They've been married since I was sixteen.) Since I lived five hundred miles away, I did not help her move this time. The next time that I visited, she was settled into the back bedroom of my aunt's house, just a short walk from where she grew up on the farm after the family moved from Akron. She had made that walk plenty of times with her sister and her mother through the woods and across the "crick" to the lake, but she was not making that walk ever again. I am sure that she felt like she was, in some way, going home. There was no mention of leaving here "feet first."

Back in Ohio, there was an MS charity bike ride called Pedal to the Point. It is a two-day, 150-mile ride from Cleveland to Sandusky, home of the famous Cedar Point Amusement Park. The ride is now called the Buckeye Breakaway. I had wanted to do it since I first heard about it many years ago but never really knew what it involved or how to raise the necessary money. I had biked for many years but wasn't a serious road cyclist. Around the time of her move, I started to train for my first MS bike ride. I had ridden a Specialized commuter bike that I had purchased at Eddy's Bike Shop in Stow, Ohio for a couple of years until some great Tennessee friends gave me a vintage 1970s Peugeot road bike. Everything began to fall into place. I began to train for the annual Bike to Jack and Back MS 150 in Middle Tennessee on my new bike. This is a two-day, 150-mile ride from Franklin to Lynchburg, home of Jack Daniel's Distillery. There are actually two routes, the long and the short. The short route is sixty-five miles each day, but I felt that I wasn't actually "doing it" unless I did the seventy-five-mile route. I started to train, riding about thirty miles at a time. I felt good after each ride and was confident that if I had to, I could do the route two more times, which was more than the total ride.

Little did I know that the bike didn't fit me properly, and I hadn't learned about the benefits of clipless shoes and pedals yet. The bike had vintage pedals with toe cages and the idea of clipless pedals scared me. For the non-cyclists, clipless pedals require cycling shoes with cleats, and the shoes lock in to the pedals with a "click" sound. If you have never used them, you will fall at least once. Guaranteed. It's part of the initiation. The downside of regular pedals is that you are wasting energy by not being clipped in during your upstroke. Clipless pedals are great for climbing hills and maintaining speed. Now, after using them for years, I can't imagine riding without them. But back then, they were scary. I rode with tennis shoes and toe cages. With trepidation, I officially registered for the ride and started to solicit pledges.

Thanks to my music fans and geography friends, I raised and exceeded the $300 minimum donation in a short amount of time as I continued to train.

This was my first real ride, and I didn't really know what I was doing, what to expect, or what I had gotten myself into. I arrived the morning of the ride with about nine hundred other cyclists in my mountain bike shorts, long-sleeved Kent State Under Armour T-shirt, tennis shoes, and unshaved legs. All around me were professional looking cyclists in spandex shorts with smooth legs, pro jerseys, and great bikes. I felt a little like my old self as a freshman at that new school with no friends. I got in the group for the long route and awaited the start of the ride. I was excited as the ride started, but I had no idea what I was in for. It was a beautiful, crisp, Tennessee morning in October as the ride headed out at 7:30 a.m.

And we were off. The Bike to Jack and Back MS 150 is a well-supported ride with rest stops about every eight to twelve miles. It's never long before you see a SAG (supply and gear) vehicle, and the rest stops all have great food, water, Gatorade, and bike mechanics. The cool morning air felt great as I rode with other riders through the misty October morning. I didn't need a break, but I stopped at the first rest stop like everyone else. There were bikes and people everywhere, but I still felt alone.

I overheard some riders talking, "Yeah, it's coming up." What was coming up? A hill. A big fucking hill. I left out of the rest stop and fumbled getting into my pedals with the toe cages. My baggy mountain bike shorts got caught on my water bottle, and it went skidding across the road. Not a good sign. I rescued my water bottle and got back on the route. I felt good but was a little apprehensive about the hill since people were talking about it. I wished that I hadn't overheard them because now it was all I could think about. I rode on and gradually approached what I thought could be the hill. This isn't so bad. It wasn't the hill. It couldn't have been it. Then I saw it—a leviathan rising out of the deep as the road snaked up a mountain. Shit. Here we go. I don't know what the grade was, but it was a serious climb. Riders were passing me at regular intervals, standing up and pedaling in their pro gear as I struggled, wasting my energy in my tennis shoes and pedals with toe cages.

I had to stop. I stopped three or four times, rested, then got back on my bike and continued to climb the hill, not realizing that it was acceptable to walk up the steep incline. As I neared the top, a female rider with incredibly muscular thighs passed me and yelled, "That's beautiful," as she looked out at the view. I reached the top and saw the view. It was incredible. I got off my bike momentarily and pulled out my disposable camera to snap a shot of the view. Otherwise, no one would believe it. Just then, an older guy rode by me and said, "Heck of a view." I said, "Yep." He said, "Not worth it." I laughed, "Nope!"

That was the toughest hill of the ride, but it still didn't get any easier. In the town of Shelbyville, I fell down. A short while later, my right ankle wasn't working right. I was tired and still had many miles to go. I was in a residential area when I got off my bike and sat near the sidewalk in front of several houses feeling somewhat defeated. I will admit that if a SAG truck came by, I would have gotten on it. I was looking for one. Waiting. One never came. I am grateful because that would have meant that I didn't finish the ride. I got back on my bike and trudged on. Many of the miles that I rode were alone. Occasionally, I encountered other riders and SAG vehicles, but more than once, I questioned whether I had made a wrong turn and was lost. I had to be the last one on the route. A SAG vehicle pulled up beside me and the driver said, "Long day in the saddle?" I uttered a breathy, "Yeah," and kept pedaling.

I had come too far to quit. But I wanted to. What the hell had I gotten myself into? Then a van approached me from the front. It looked like my mom's van with the wheelchair lift and hand controls, and I remembered why I was riding. I kept going. The last stretch of the Bike to Jack and Back is an insulting, smack-in-the-face, piss-you-off, gradual climb that never seems to end. You're so close to the finish line, and the hill just keeps going and going. It sucks. All you can do is keep pedaling. My thighs hurt. I was hungry. My neck hurt. My butt hurt. I had to pee. My wrists and back were sore. My ankle wasn't working. Then I saw it. The finish line. There is an intersection about a quarter mile before the end of the trek and I found it odd that there was another rider there, stopped, who seemed to be in very good shape. He was resting and breathing hard. I wasn't last! Halle-fuckin-lujah! After seventy-five miles on a vintage road bike that didn't fit me, wearing tennis shoes and pedals with toe cages, I crossed the finish line alone with little to no fanfare. I didn't ride the next day. It was too much, and I felt fortunate that I made it the whole seventy-five miles on day one.

The Bike to Jack and Back ride was in October and as November crept on, something inside of me was telling me to go to Ohio for Thanksgiving. I decided to plan a surprise visit, after confirming with my aunt that my mom's weak and frail body could take the shock of me arriving unannounced. We pulled it off perfectly. I came over in the morning a couple days before Thanksgiving, walked back to my mom's room and casually asked, "So what's for breakfast?" She stared at me. She blinked her eyes, smiled with a puzzled look on her face and said, "What are you doing here?" I just laughed. "Are you surprised?" "Yeah!" she said, as if that was an obviously stupid question. A short while later as I sat beside her bed, she looked at me and said, "Golly!" which was her signature word when she was sincerely shocked. "So why are you here?" "To see you," I said. She was silent and just looked at me. Though she was unable to leave her bed and join the rest of the family for Thanksgiving dinner, we truly had a good time, and I was glad to see that she was doing much better than when she was living alone in the apartment. As we talked, she said, "Well, you finally did it," referring to the MS bike ride. I said, "Yeah, but not really." She asked, "What do you mean?" I said, "I only rode the first day." She fired back, "You did it! You finished!" That made me feel good. I did do it. I did finish.

-9-

Johnny Marzetti

Most people around the world know that Nashville is the capital of country music. Just take a stroll along lower Broadway among the honky-tonk tourist traps, cowboy hats, and rivers of Bud Light, and you will quickly understand why the city is sometimes referred to as NashVegas. But it is so much more than that. There are plenty of reputable rock, hip-hop, jazz, and singer-songwriters that are definitively and defiantly not country (at least what is known as country music today). Even though the vast majority of the songs on the charts that are written about trucks, tailgates, dirt roads, moonlight, and country girls in tight shorts are sung by smiling, sanitized "country boys," many are written in Music Row writing rooms by men in their forties. And these guys aren't riding around town in pickup trucks. Outside of the formulaic dreck that represents Nashville on country radio and the infinite parade of award shows, artists like Peter Frampton, Ben Folds, and Dave Mustaine are just a few of the non-country entertainers that call Music City home. In addition to music, Nashville has become a popular location for major motion pictures, well before the former ABC drama series that shares the city's name was created. I told you all that so I could tell you this:

Cherry blossoms in bloom on 1st Avenue N., Nashville, TN

Before moving to Nashville, I had a very small part in a well-produced indie film called the *Path of the Wind* that was shot in Cleveland, Ohio. The movie, which received a few modest awards, featured a cameo appearance by Wilford Brimley, and despite my never actually seeing the finished product, I got a little bite from the acting bug.

In Nashville in early 2010, I submitted for a background part posted on Craigslist for a major production company. Nashville's Craigslist isn't the joke that it is in some other cities. At this point, I had already been an extra in a few productions and was used to not hearing back regarding a submission. I sent off my information and forgot about it. A few weeks later, I got a callback for a part in a new film with Gwyneth Paltrow and Tim McGraw. The working title was "Love, Don't Let Me Down." I was almost embarrassed to tell anyone that I was involved in a film with such a stupid name. (That was probably the idea to keep the production quiet.) The movie would ultimately be called "Country Strong." It didn't do too well at the box office, even though it was a pretty good film, despite my obvious bias. The story was dark and didn't have a happy ending, so that's probably the reason it didn't get better reviews.

I remember getting the call from casting that I got the part as a "Backstage VIP" in a scene with the above-mentioned stars. I was excited, but the shoot was on a day that we had scheduled a long weekend in Ohio. I had already spoken with my mom and aunt and assured them that we would be in town. I knew that she had very little to look forward to, and I hated to have to break my plans to visit. When she was living in the house or the apartment in Newton Falls, I often called and changed my plans, and I felt bad about those times. I told the woman from casting that I didn't think I could do it because I would be out of town, but thanked her for calling, feeling disappointed but morally confident that I was making the right decision. With no ulterior motives, I called my mom shortly after to tell her that I got a call to be in the movie, but filming was on the date that I was planning to visit, so I turned it down.

She said, "Are you crazy?! Why would you not do it?!"

I said, "Because I am coming to see you."

She said, "Do it!"

It reminded me of some of my early gigs when she used to tell me that "you never know who is in the audience." I never forgot that.

I responded, "Really? You don't care?"

She ordered, "No! You can't pass this up! Are you crazy!?"

I was so relieved that she wanted me to do the shoot and that she wasn't upset about the change of plans. I called the number on my phone and got the voice mail for the casting office. I left a message and called my mom back to tell her. We were both excited as we discussed this opportunity and how I was happy that she was ok with me doing it when my phone beeped with an incoming call. I told her it was them and with animated excitement she said, "Call me back!" For a moment, it felt like old times when she would be happy for me if I got a local gig or made some great contact at a show. I told the casting director that I could do the shoot, we exchanged the necessary information, and I was scheduled to be in the scene. I called my mother back and told her the details, and we both laughed about the frequency of phone calls. I felt good that I had honestly tried to do the right thing by turning down the part and felt even better that she was supporting and encouraging me in doing what I wanted to do. Dopamine and adrenaline were coursing through my system. Life was good.

We eventually rescheduled the visit, and it was clear that Aunt Marty was overwhelmed. My mom's nursing aides came every day for several hours. She had a small bell that she rang when she needed or wanted something, and she did not hesitate to use it. Whenever my aunt left the house for a shopping trip, to go out for dinner or to visit friends, my mom called on her cell phone to ask when she was coming home. Aunt Marty had an older husband to take care of, not to mention herself. More than once, she called me late in the evening, crying because she did not know what to do. The doctors could not do much to help my mom. She was diagnosed with osteoporosis after breaking a vertebra, which was fused, and a pain pump was installed. When I was there last, she asked me, "You know that saying 'God only gives you what you can handle?' Well, I don't know how much I am supposed to handle." One night, she went to the hospital in an ambulance with lights and sirens blaring because she was so ill. Her speech was difficult to understand; her memory and cognitive abilities were fading.

It was not long after this visit that Aunt Marty called.

When the phone rang, I knew it wasn't good. I could just feel it. No unexpected late-night call is ever good when you are an adult. She told me that she was moving my mom to a nursing home. This was a very difficult decision for my aunt, and looking back, if it wasn't her making it, it would have probably had to have been me at some point. She told me that she had researched several places and found one that she felt good about. My mom didn't know yet, and she told me not to say anything. She was distraught, and I assured her that she was doing the right thing. She cried. Once again, I felt helpless and alone. I didn't know when my aunt would tell her, but I knew it would be soon.

One of the next few times I talked to my mom on the phone, I told her I wasn't sure what I would be doing over the summer. In a small and fragile voice, she said, "You can come and take care of me." Obviously, my aunt had told her, but she didn't know that I knew. I said, "I wish I could," with an unusual tone, and subconsciously, I think we both knew that the other knew. The next time we talked, she told me what was going on. I acted surprised like I didn't know and asked the details. I told her I understood and wished that I could do something. I don't remember the exact conversation. It was hard to hear. But I do recall her saying, in a monotone voice, "Aunt Marty can't take care of me anymore." I don't believe that she was upset or nonunderstanding. She needed more care than her sister could provide, and she wasn't getting any better. And she knew that she wasn't getting any better. I do believe that she felt this was the end for her.

I continued to talk to my father on a regular basis and had somewhat of a normal relationship. At least as normal as could be expected. Not too long before this event, he had offered to drive my sister and me to Ohio to visit for a weekend. Obviously, I had seen my mother frequently, but this was about his daughter seeing her mother, and I am sure that I was being used as some sort of buffer. Either way, I said, "Sure. Just let me know when." I wanted my mom to see her daughter because I knew that it would make her happy, and it sounded like a great opportunity to repair some old wounds inside the confines of a motor vehicle for five hundred miles. Or to kill one another. As I agreed to the trip, I could envision myself stranded on the roadside of northbound I-65 with my thumb out. He estimated a date. That date came and went without any mention, explanation, or apology. After some time passed, I inquired about when the trip might happen so that I could make plans and was told, "We're going to wait until she's settled into the nursing home." Thanks for letting me know. The trip never happened.

We started to make plans to help out with my mom's transition to the new residence. She was concerned about not having a phone in the nursing home and not having immediate contact with people. We bought her a cell phone and preprogrammed it so that she would only have to press one number to call any of us. She was still worried about how she would physically get to the phone since she was bedridden and couldn't reach it if it was on a dresser or table. Kerri sewed a bag with Velcro straps that hung on the rails of the hospital bed to store the phone so she could access it at any time.

It was from that phone that I got the last voice mail message that I would ever receive from her. I was teaching an evening class at Columbia State, and I noticed a message on my phone just as my class was beginning. On the break, I checked my messages, and it was from my mom. Her speech was clearer than I had heard it in years. "I just wanted to say 'thank you' for the phone. It's really great." If there was more than that, it wasn't much because that is all I remember. Either way, it was more than enough. I was happy and sad all at the same time.

The days leading up to making the trip to help move her belongings from my aunt's house, I started getting some strange thoughts and feelings. Overall, it was a feeling of "say what you need to say." I can't explain it, but I knew there were some things that I needed to tell my mother. Nothing bad or secretive, just to convey certain ways that I felt or didn't say enough.

We arrived at my aunt's house to help after my mom had made the move to the nursing home, but the majority of her belongings were still there, and we needed to go through them. It is difficult going through a loved one's personal belongings after they have died, but it is very surreal doing it while they are very much among the living. My aunt told me that my mom had said to her, "Don't just throw my things away." Ugh. I could hear her voice in my head, and it broke my heart. It still does. "Things" were important to my mom. Not just the mundane accumulation of them, but rather, who gave them to you, why and the sentimental value. I couldn't imagine just throwing her things away.

We began sorting through her remaining possessions. Some things brought back memories, some items I never knew she had, and some were just funny. I kept the vintage midcentury, accordion-style sewing chest that I remember from when I was a child, just barely tall enough to reach it. It was an old, 1960s-era, foldable sewing chest with multiple compartments, and I am sure that the majority of the thread in it is older than me. It's not worth any money, and I don't know where she got it, but it's been in my life as long as I can remember. It is actually a pretty cool design, and I still have it today with a lot of the same little items still in it: sewing needles, spools of thread, patches, a vintage yellow, plastic measuring tape for fabric, and thimbles. (It's surprising that I didn't end up a tailor of some sort for as much as I was fascinated by thimbles when I was a kid.) She had school-related books of my grandmother's from when she was a kid. I will never forget the slam book where someone had written to my grandmother, "I'll love you 'til Eskimos wear B.V.Ds." You can't forget that. And receipts. She had receipts from my grandmother buying a load of coal in 1965. Receipts from my grandmother's rent payments to her brother who owned her house. She had the receipt from her first car and just about every electronic purchase she had ever made. Not to mention the warranty cards and owner's manuals for those electronic devices that she didn't even have anymore. I kept a few of the more interesting paper archives, but the majority was trash. Faded ink on thermal paper. Since she couldn't wear "regular" clothes anymore, her clothing went to the Salvation Army or my aunt's garage sale. Her wardrobe for the last year or so was nightgowns that had been cut up the back like a hospital gown. Her van sat idle outside, slowly becoming one with the soil. Other than some books, a small loveseat, and her jewelry boxes, that was about it. I made sure that I got her photo albums that dated back to before I was born. She got rid of her furniture and other large items when she moved from the apartment.

This was a strange time. I didn't really know what or how to feel. The ride from my mother-in-law's house to my aunt's place is a scenic, pastoral trip that winds through West Branch State Park; at least it is the way that I go. These are roads that my friends and I would drink and drive on, discovering the roots of rock and roll, all while attempting to solve the world's problems. My ride there was a calm, short journey of contemplation and introspection. The opening track on *The Glass Passenger* by Jack's Mannequin started the soundtrack of my unaccompanied, rural ride. I drove with the windows down despite the cold air on roads that I couldn't wait to leave when I was younger but now could never forget. Random words and phrases in the songs "Crashin'" and "Spinning" connected with me and my thoughts. I felt like I was crashing, and the world seemed to be spinning out of control around me. But the song "Swim" is what really hit me. It's a song about hope, courage, and strength. Don't give up, just keep your head above water, and swim.

My first visit with her in the nursing home was as uncomfortable as could be expected. She was silent most of the time, expressionless, and I don't think that she smiled. Who could blame her? She was in a fucking nursing home, for Christ's sake. All things considered, the place was fairly nice. It didn't have that "nursing home smell," and the hallways and common areas resembled more of a retirement home than a nursing facility. By definition, the place was a long-term care facility with skilled nursing, rehab, and Alzheimer's care. There was a "fine dining" restaurant and a beauty salon on location. They had programs and events like bingo, trivia, karaoke, line dancing, and trips to the zoo. The nurse's station was outside of my mom's room, just in case you needed reminding of where you were.

We sat, talking. About what, I don't remember. But I do remember that while we were there, they brought in her supper. They lifted the lid on the tray to reveal a bowl of what looked like congealed tomato soup. The paper menu that accompanied it said it was Johnny Marzetti—a pasta casserole with cheese, ground beef, and tomato sauce. It usually resembles lasagna, but with elbow macaroni. I honestly looked for something else under the large dish that she was supposed to add to it. Nope. That was it. I was traumatized. She was on a pureed diet because of swallowing issues, and this was her dinner. I do not recall ever feeling so heartbroken and distraught.

For a very long time, food has made me sad. I don't really know why, but maybe it has to do with choice. Choosing what you want to eat. Maybe it's because of the essence of life-sustaining nourishment, and I am aware that many go without, while so many people in the developed world overeat and waste food daily. Or maybe it was because every time we ate supper at my grandma's when I was younger, my mom used to say, "Well, eat hearty, because there's nothing at home." Then she'd laugh. I didn't think it was funny. When we went to wedding receptions, graduation parties, or family picnics at the lake, she always sent me to get her a plate of food. "You know what I like," she would always say. I did. I always felt bad for her having to suffer through those Mobile Meals. She was so happy about a hamburger that my aunt once made for her while she was living there. Simple, but so good. Especially after all those years of delivered meals, fast food, and leftovers. There is no comparison to a homecooked meal. Now her meals were blended, institutional goop.

During our visit, I awkwardly told her that I was glad that I went with her after the divorce. After all, I did have a choice, and I had sometimes thought about what my life would have been like if I had gone to live with my father. Just thinking about having gone with him makes me want to wipe my hands on my shirt like George Bailey in *It's a Wonderful Life* after he shook Mr. Potter's hand. Dirty. My mom just looked at me. But I felt better after telling her that going with her after the divorce was the right decision for me.

There were a few good things that happened here. She had her first real shower in several years. Because so many residents are elderly and are in wheelchairs, the facility has a sit-down shower. She also had her hair done at the beauty salon. Uncle Howard visited her in the nursing home, and I was told he just sat there and held her hand the whole time. I don't ever remember him saying too much anyway. He and his wife did not have children, and he treated my mom and her siblings like his own. He remembered her being born, and here she was, in his words, "on her last legs."

We came to visit again the next day. She wasn't in her room. The nurse said that she was in the TV room. We made our way to the community television room, where my eyes searched the sea of expressionless, aged faces for my mother. Many were in wheelchairs, and it was as if most of these bodies had simply been parked there. I felt like I was walking through a crowd of people who were wearing masks. Strange faces that didn't really look alive. The TV was loud. No one was talking. Then I saw my mom at the far end of the room, slumped over in her wheelchair, asleep. We walked over to her and carefully woke her. How anyone could sleep in this environment is beyond me.

She didn't smile and looked at me almost as if she didn't know me. She said, "Push me over there." It was a small space adjacent to the main room.

"I wish you got here twenty minutes ago."

"Why?"

"They dropped me."

"What do you mean they dropped you?"

"They *dropped* me. They were moving me from the bed to my chair and they dropped me."

It was in her chart that the staff was to use a Hoyer lift sling to transport her from the bed to her wheelchair. According to her, they did not use the sling, and they dropped her on the floor. Of course, none of the staff would admit to this, and I am honestly not sure if it happened. I had no reason to disbelieve her, but maybe she imagined it, or she created the story. I'll never know. But I certainly did not know what to do. Once again, I felt helpless. I got the nurse and got her back to her room. When we got her back to the room, she was emotionless and somber. We had to head home the next day and reluctantly left so she could get some rest.

-10-
Don't Talk to That Man

Back home in Tennessee, I taught my classes, worked out, drank Scotch, wrote my music, drank more Scotch, and felt confident that, for better or worse, the situation was the best it could be. We had done the right thing. It seemed like everything was going well in the nursing home, which is why I was so surprised when I got the call. Part of her routine care was the cleaning and changing of the supra pubic catheter. Her home health care aides had done it since she was in the apartment in Newton Falls, and there hadn't been any problems. Apparently, while changing her catheter one morning in the nursing home, the nurse punctured her bowel. My mother heard a rushing of air and said, "What was that?" The nurse replied, "Just some gas" and carried on with the procedure. My mom knew something was wrong. She called my aunt on the cell phone. "They did something. I know something's wrong." She alerted the staff, who did almost nothing for over four hours. They then called an ambulance to take her to the hospital.

After four hours with a hole in her large intestine and nothing done, the news was not good. She was septic. They admitted her to the intensive care unit. It wasn't long after when I got a call from my aunt telling

My mom (*right*) and her sister Marty on 7th Avenue in Akron.

me that they were talking about putting her on a respirator and a feeding tube. What the hell happened? That's all we could think. How could she have gone from showing improvement and participating in social functions to needing life support in the ICU? It was a Monday evening. We left for Ohio the next day.

We packed clothes for a few days and nights. I have no memory of the trip or of getting there. I mainly remember walking into the hospital and seeing her in the ICU. There was no real door to her room, just a curtain. The intensive care unit was an open area with constant activity. Machines, wires, tubes, beeps, and flashing LEDs. It all could have been from a movie set. She was wearing a BiPAP mask, which made it all the more surreal. Much later, I learned that "BiPAP" is an acronym for Bi-level Positive Airway Pressure. It's a breathing machine. A ventilator. She had also been diagnosed with mild pneumonia while in the hospital. It was hard to talk to her because of the machine, and she kept trying to take the mask off. There was a strange smell. Not bad, not good, but not like anything I had ever smelled before. I tried to talk to her, but it was difficult. She couldn't speak well, and I couldn't hear her anyway because of the noise of the breathing machine. Her mouth was very dry, and she was NPO (nil per os / Latin for "nothing by mouth").

All she wanted was a drink of water. So simple and pure. Water. Life doesn't exist without it. We waste it. We pollute it. We take it for granted every day. But it was not permissible. She said that her throat felt like she had swallowed broken glass. When the nurse came by to moisten her mouth with a small sponge on a stick, she aggressively bit it and sucked the water out of it. Right away, the doctors and nurses conveyed that the news was not good. She had been exposed to the toxins for too long, and her body was too weak from the advanced MS to fight the trauma. She was basically on life support.

She drifted in and out of lucidity and in between ramblings, I tried to talk to her. She had strange, sporadic thoughts, probably from the meds and because she was getting all of her nutrients from a temporary tube. As my aunt arrived one morning, my mom asked her with wide, fearful eyes, "Who got killed?!" "Nobody got killed," she replied. Later that day when I was there, she kept asking about a man out in the hallway. "Who is that? Who is that man?" she would ask. There was no one there. My great-uncle Victor, her father's brother, had recently died, and my aunt was convinced that she was seeing his ghost in the hallway. She saw him a few more times. Later, as I was leaving to go get something to eat, I told her that I would be back soon. She said to me as I left, "Don't talk to that man." "I won't," I said.

Time seemed to stop. One day blurred into the next. I didn't sleep much. Fatigue and hunger were constant, yet nonexistent. She seemed oblivious, but she was aware of much more than I realized. When her doctor came by for his rounds, he said to her in a jovial tone, "So, Shirley, how are you feeling?" *My god*, I thought, *he thinks he is seeing another patient*, and I felt terribly bad for my mom that he had made a mistake. Not to mention that maybe she had been getting some else's care. She just looked at him with an amused smirk. It was a joke that started before I got there; he was calling her Shirley MacLaine (Betty "McClain."). Indeed, she probably understood much more than we thought. But it was hard to tell during the times when she was hallucinating or thinking she was somewhere else. One time she said to me, "If you want to ask me a question, please don't tap me on the top of the head." I had never touched her head. I said, "Okay, I won't."

Over the course of a few days, the numbers on her machines kept going up and down. Good and bad. At one point she said, "So what are we gonna do for supper?" Supper. How I wished that we were all at my grandma's or Aunt Ruth's or out for a shopping trip and needed to decide what we were going to eat for dinner. Maybe some pizza from Mama Joe's in Kent or even a bag of little burgers from the Hamburger Station in Akron. Another time, she looked sternly at my wife and me and demanded, "I want you two to get marriage counseling!" We couldn't help but laugh. She also randomly exclaimed to all of us, "Let's put our heads together" with a strange look on her face. Another time she blurted out, "heads up!" She talked and rambled about racial prejudice, religion, and the plight of same-sex couples and lamented "that's what they're teaching 'em!" My mom was not a racist, homophobe, or Jesus freak. She believed everyone had the right to do their own thing, as long as it didn't hurt others. For some reason, her brain was firing off about people who taught their children to hate.

She also asked if later we all could get something "substantial" to eat. My heart sank. She was hungry. At some point, the doctor came back around and started discussing the fact that she was not getting better, and we might want to consider hospice. The alternative was a feeding tube—full life support. Though her hearing was compromised by the din of the BiPAP machine, and she was not entirely conscious, I was uneasy with the conversation and felt that it was grossly inconsiderate to discuss this matter right in front of her. I asked that we step out to the hallway. "Sure," the doctor said, and we filed out of the room. Shouldn't he have had that sense as a care provider? I asked him what hospice entailed and specifically asked about the nutrition tube. He said, "No nutrition." I felt a pit in my stomach.

After this discussion, I went back in and sat with her. "You know, you really got screwed."

She looked at me and said, "You mean life?"

I said, "Yep."

She rolled her eyes as if to say, "You think?"

I told her that I respected her for doing what she needed to do to get free. She took a huge chance. She could have passively spent her life in an unhappy marriage, played it safe and been taken care of, but she chose to go her own way, to enjoy what quality time she had. I remember when I was a teenager, she frequently quoted lyrics from Billy Joel's "My Life" and raised her voice as she sang "Leave Me Alone."

She explained to me that she had talked to her best friend from high school prior to asking for a divorce. She was thirty-five years old, and her plan was to wait until she was forty. Her friend told her, "You can't wait." Then my mom's voice trailed off. That was all I needed to hear.

Sometime later I asked, "Are you mad at me?"

Puzzled, she looked at me with concern. "No. Why?"

I said, "For moving." I needed to know that she didn't resent me for leaving Ohio.

She looked at me with serious and sincere eyes. "I'm glad you moved!"

Taken out of context, that sounds bad, but the look on her face and the tone in her weak voice was positive. I said, "Because I would never have been in that movie if I didn't." (As if that was the only thing, but it was the most recent and biggest she knew about.) She agreed, and it made me feel that my decision was okay with her.

Though we were not on speaking terms, I felt it necessary to inform my sister that her mother was gravely ill. After the first day of being there, I explained to her on the phone in no uncertain terms that she needed to get to the hospital because the situation was dire. She took her time getting there and basically questioned my explanation of her condition. I didn't care if I ever saw her again, but I wanted my mother to see her daughter once more before she died. We needed to tell my mother the circumstances and begin hospice care. She was suffering, and the nurses wanted to know what was taking so long. They wanted to know when "the daughter was going to get here." One of them commented, "We've seen this many times. She's probably waiting for the weekend." I was concerned that my mother couldn't hang on much longer. Her numbers were not good. After some time had passed, I asked her carefully, "Mom, do you want to see your daughter?" She replied, "Yeah....But I can't go there."

It took my sister and her family three days to get from Georgia to Ohio, even though it usually takes about thirteen hours on the road or a little over an hour in the air. That was the weekend. I will not include the uncomfortable details of how difficult her initial interaction was with everyone upon arriving. She exited the elevator on the floor and acted as if she didn't see us in the hallway. She talked with the nurses rather than us and tried to force her way into my mom's room unannounced. Because she had refused to take me seriously on the phone, the solemnity of the situation seemed to defeat her arrogant attitude, and she suddenly became somewhat of a concerned daughter. Somewhat. We included her in every discussion with the doctors, nurses, and hospice caregivers, but she deferred all decisions to me and my aunt, saying "whatever y'all decide." She was persistently passive, except when it came to invoking her biased religious beliefs. We spoke with the doctors, nurses, and hospice and decided that it was time to tell my mom that there was nothing more they could do.

We had only been waiting for my sister to arrive. Now that she was here, and we got beyond her problematic nature, we all talked about what needed to be said and officially enter hospice. As the elder child, I felt it was my responsibility and obligation to tell my mom the truth of the situation. Furthermore, she had raised me through my adolescence as a single parent, and I had been her caregiver for many years. I felt that my aunt had done more than could ever be expected of her after moving my mother into her home, giving full access to the nurses and caregivers, and securing the nursing home that was responsible for putting her in this situation. My aunt asked her, "Betty, do you want to be put on a feeding tube?" My mom nodded "yes." She then told her, "You know, that means you won't be able to eat again, and you'll be attached to machines." She looked at us and slowly shook her head "no" with a straight, expressionless face.

After the conversation, I went in to talk to her. At this point I was on autopilot. I didn't think about the words, they just came out. I sat down beside her bed. The theater in my mind has me holding her hand, but I don't remember if I did or not. My skin crawled. I felt like my head was in a vice. All my clothes suddenly shrank and became too tight. It was hot. The only words that I truly remember saying were "I wish I had all of the money in the world," as if that could have made a difference. She looked at me as I spoke. In so many words, I said that the doctors had done all that they could do for her. She stopped me. In her labored voice, she calmly said to me, "I think this is a conversation...that I need to have with my sister." Though I was prepared to follow through no matter how difficult this was, I was a bit relieved in two ways. Obviously, the pressure was off in explaining to her that she was dying, but maybe more importantly, my mother was protecting me. She didn't want me to have to go through the painful experience of explaining this to her. I was still a kid.

It all happened so fast. The machines were switched off. Wires were quickly disconnected. The BiPap mask was removed. The curtain was pulled back, her bed was wheeled out, and we all headed for the elevator. Hospice was on the next floor up in the hospital. The gurney went feet first in the elevator, and we all crowded in. My sister was the last one, and it looked as though she wouldn't fit. She said, "I'll wait." I could not bear the thought of her not being included in the journey to the next floor, and I forced her into the congested elevator. The hospice floor was calm. The lights were dim, and it was quiet. I think in all of our minds, hospice was a countdown, and the clock just started.

We would soon learn that this was not the case. It felt like something should happen. But nothing happened.

We settled into my mom's room on the next floor. She was well aware what was going on and made a few heartbreaking comments, though she was not sad, upset, or scared. She had recently had her nails done at the nursing home, and before we moved upstairs to hospice, she noted that one was chipped. She calmly said, "Well, I guess it doesn't matter now." As she was lying in bed being moved into her room, something happened to some of the equipment, and she commented, "I even screw up my own death." She had an oxygen mask, a catheter, and an IV port for pain medication. Dilaudid and Ativan pumped into her veins from the IV. The former is a strong pain killer, and the latter is a sedative used to treat anxiety disorders. We had met with the head hospice nurse, and she explained what hospice was like. A lot of what she said to us seemed rehearsed and a bit routine. She gave us brochures and pamphlets that attempted to explain different behaviors and events. I felt like a customer. My mom soon became unconscious but was aware of much that was going on.

There was a strange calm that came over all of us. A weird sense of relief. We talked and joked about some of the things that she said over the last couple days. "Heads up!" and "let's put our heads together!" made her smile, silent, eyes closed. My cousin Beth arrived at some point, and I told her about the "marriage counseling" comment. She said, "I've got a cooler full of 'counseling' out in the car." She smiled at that, too. She drifted in and out of consciousness and when she was awake, she mostly talked to her sister. The day turned to evening and we had all been in and out the room many times.

The room was dim. I was standing at the foot of the bed while my aunt was at her side talking and tending to her.

My mom asked, "Who's that?"

Aunt Marty answered, "That's Stephen!"

"My son's name is Stephen!" she said.

If it wasn't for the fatigue and mental exhaustion, I probably would have lost it.

She soon became unconscious but was still aware of much of what was going on. The first night was rough. We all agreed to not leave her alone for the night, and Kerri and I volunteered to stay. I can only say good things about the hospice program at the hospital. Nurses were in the room on a regular schedule and were available when we needed anything. Despite the nurses, we "worked" all night long. Even though the trifold pamphlets had warned us what would happen, we were still not prepared. In an unconscious state, she tried to remove her oxygen mask, talked, yelled, mumbled, and pulled at imaginary strings in the air. It was constant. She moaned. She told me, "Put me over there." I said, "Okay. There. Is that better?" It was. (I hadn't done anything.) She yelled for a friend who had lived in the apartment building in Newton Falls. She went on and on, mostly not making any sense, telling odd stories, and asking questions. At one point, she stopped rambling and asked, "So how was your day?" Staggered amid responding to her babbling, I half smiled and said, "It was good. How was your day?" She answered in a sincere, lilting voice, "It was fantastic!" I can still hear her voice and the way that she emphasized the second syllable of the word. It makes me wonder sometimes if what we are experiencing right now is even real; she was somewhere else. Somewhere good. Somewhere fantastic.

We were exhausted when the sun came up. The coming days would be even more exhausting. I kept getting this feeling that I needed to stay there. There was a balcony not far from her room that I would go out on for fresh air, and I would get a sense of walking off it. Not to jump and harm myself, just walking off. Like a giant. Strange. We spent most of our time at the hospital either with her or somewhere in the building. The nurses brought a cart of doughnuts and breakfast items every morning, and I gained a good ten pounds. We ate in the hospital cafeteria or got takeout. I refused to eat in her room because I didn't want her to have to smell it, so we ate in the small kitchenette around the corner. I remember as a kid having a casual discussion about dying (because that happens!), and she said that she just didn't want to starve to death. I feared that's what was happening. Sometimes I sat in the chapel down the hall. We were a regular fixture on the floor—that is, my wife, my aunt, and me.

As I said before, I didn't care if I ever saw my sister again, but I wanted my mother to see her second-born child. She stayed three days and left without saying goodbye to anyone but me. The reason? Her husband had to get back to work, and she had to get her kids back in school. I was dumbfounded when she told me she was leaving. I suggested she let the others go, and she could stay with us. Ride with us. Get a plane ticket. Figure it out as you go. After all, that's what we were all doing. We had jobs, too. She and I stood at the elevator, and I told her that "you can't get this time back." The elevator door closed. I went back in the room and told everyone that she left. We never saw her again.

This country has a strange relationship with mortality. I think many will agree that we live in a death-denying culture. We catalog our elderly and infirm away in compounds that are disconnected from the mainstream. An old folks' "home." A retirement "community." The entertainment industry deifies youth over experience. Old people are often portrayed in films and television as being confused, irrelevant, withdrawn, or incapable of physical activity. My mom had acted older than her years for quite some time because of the people she was around. She started to act like the old hens that lived in the apartment building. Now, in a strange way, she was young again. She was her old self, even though her eyes were closed, and she only communicated with moans and grunts. Maybe because there were no more excuses. There was nothing more to hide. The ugly truth, whatever that was. And just like it had been for so long, it was just her and me. I talked to her like things were normal. There was generally no response. I held her hand and asked her to squeeze if she could hear me. Slowly and faintly, her hand weakly gripped mine. She could hear what I was saying. She was still here.

She used to joke about the fact that I was never baptized as a baby. Good. That's a decision that should be made by each individual. I don't really even know what it means, but it apparently bothered my mom enough that she brought it up on many occasions. There was a preacher that was there since the beginning of our hospital stay. Preacher, minister, reverend, father—I don't really know the difference between any of the monikers. As comedian Bill Burr said in one of his stand-up bits on religion, "it's just some guy." Regardless, he was pretty cool. I mentioned to him that I had never been baptized and he said that he could do that. Okay. I knew it would make my mom happy to know that I wouldn't float around for the rest of whatever. We made the arrangements for me to be baptized. The preacher explained to me that "you don't have to go to church every Sunday. You just need to accept Christ." Okay. So we proceeded. I held my mom's hand as he recited the words of the ceremony. I barely remember it. He then asked if I accepted Jesus Christ as my savior. I paused, obviously a little too long because he looked up. I said yes. He said some more words. And when he was finished, I got a certificate.

Every night that we drove back from the hospital to my mother-in-law's house, I popped open a cold Great Lakes beer and drank it on the way. When it was empty, I threw the bottle out the car window at a speed limit sign like we used to do when I was in high school. Back then, I could hit a sign with the accuracy of a major-league pitcher striking out a batter with a loud, metallic crack and the sound of breaking glass. In my mind, I was playing a game. If I missed, my mom would live another day. I didn't hit a single sign on those nights. We officially had a total of three weeks' time in the hospice program. After that, arrangements had to be made for the patient to go home or be moved to a nursing facility. My mom used every last day. Probably because she wanted to get what was owed to her. She was like that. Take it if you can. She wanted everything and anything she could get. Probably the result of growing up with very little.

I was still responsible for the classes that I was teaching back in Tennessee. Since my classes only met one day a week, I actually considered driving home, teaching class, and coming back to Ohio the next day, which was not realistic. I emailed my students and higher-ups to let them know that I had personal issues to deal with. It was none of their goddamn business.

Nearing the end of the three-week period, my aunt awoke after we all spent the night in the dark hospital room. As if on cue, she arose, collected her purse, and without looking up said, "That's it. I can't take it anymore." She left. She was emotionally shot. We all were, for that matter. The staff had repeatedly told us that we needed to get some rest. No matter how much time we spent there, we would not be prepared for the end. The nurses said that we couldn't control what would happen. If we were meant to be there when she died, we would be. If not, then we wouldn't be. I don't know that I favored one or the other. I just felt an obligation. I didn't want her to be alone.

That day, we took the advice of the hospice nurses. We went to my mother-in-law's, got showers, and rested. I don't remember what we did that day because we were on autopilot. Our brains were numb. Later in the afternoon, I stopped by Aunt Marty's house, and we just visited for a while. We all tried to recharge, clear our heads, and get some rest. We decided to head back to the hospital around 5:00 p.m. The part of Northeast Ohio where my aunt lived is in a rural area about forty minutes away from the hospital. We decided to take the long way.

The scenic route. It was springtime in Ohio, and it was a beautiful April afternoon. Blue skies, budding trees, and flowers poking through the loamy topsoil. We cracked open a couple of beers and took our time on old back roads that we all used to drink on when we were in high school. We commented on the changes, the bumpy, pothole filled roads, and the springtime vegetation. It was enjoyable in an anxious kind of way. For just a little while, nothing mattered but the springtime air, the beers, the music, and each other. Time passed, and we drove. We weren't too far from the hospital when my cell phone rang. It was the head hospice nurse. My mom had died.

I don't remember the nurse's exact words, but it didn't matter. My mom was gone. We walked into the hospital and before we took the elevator up, I called my sister. I didn't spend that much time talking. I just told her that our mother had died. I needed to get upstairs and quite honestly, I felt that I had done all that was required of me, since she chose not to be there. But looking back, in her defense, maybe she just didn't care. We arrived on the floor and the nurses prevented us from walking in the room. Calmly, we told them that we knew. They ushered us into the room. There, my mother lay. Her eyes closed and mouth slightly open. As they warned us, we were not prepared. We cried. Without even wanting to. This shouldn't have been a surprise, but it seemed unreal. The nurses assured us that she wasn't alone when she died. There was nothing more for us to do. I leaned down and kissed her forehead. Her body was still warm. I don't know why I did it. It was nothing I ever did when she was alive. Maybe I should have.

We left the room and went to the hospital chapel. I don't know why we did that either. It just seemed like what we should do. Maybe because it was peaceful. There was an open bible on a low table. We both guessed you were supposed to kneel in front of it, so we did. There on the open page read:

> Now the time came for Elizabeth to be delivered, and she gave birth to a son.

I don't know what it means, but it was weird, and it seemed like a bizarre coincidence. We both cried. Later, we met with the lead hospice nurse to discuss what was next and I told her about the passage. She said, "There are no coincidences" and gave me some religious literature. Again, I felt like a customer. I never read it. I explained to her that I was agnostic. She said, "Don't spend your life searching." I am still not sure what that is supposed to mean. After my aunt arrived and went through the same process and stages that we did, the three of us went to dinner and toasted my mom with shots of Jim Beam.

-11-

Is That All There Is?

I got out of the car at my mother-in-law's house, took out my cell phone and deleted my mother's contact. My soul was empty. I had nothing to give. No energy, no words, and no fucks. Again, in some weird way, I felt like I needed to stay there. I made plans to have dinner with an old friend—my first friend. I remember being about five years old playing alone with Matchbox cars in my grandmother's marigold garden when a boy named Tim materialized and nervously said, "I'm here to play with a boy named Stephen." We have remained in contact for most of our lives, though we really have little in common other than a shared childhood and a love of heavy metal music. Still, it's good to have those people. Dinner was awkward, and whatever it was that I was looking for, I did not get.

My mother's wish was to be cremated, but before this could happen, we had to ID her body at the funeral home. We all arrived together, and Aunt Marty said that she would do it. After viewing her sister's body, she said to me, "It's really not bad if you want to see her." I went in. Her mouth was closed, and the light was dim. She looked peaceful and twenty years younger. I slowly approached, carefully touched her shoulder, and turned and walked away. We headed back to Tennessee the next day and for eight hours and five hundred miles, I uttered not a single word and didn't even listen to the radio.

The thought of giving a lecture seemed as daunting to me as leaping across the Ohio river. I did not have the energy. Leaning against the whiteboard in front of the class, I told my students where I had been and what had happened. I can only imagine how uncomfortable that was for them. We only had a couple weeks of classes left, and I explained to them that I would not be lecturing but we would watch some topical films and do some map exercises in class.

I showed a film on that first night back, and after the class had left, I noticed a sheet of paper left behind on a student's desk. To this day, I still have the letter. For a traditional college-age student, her words were wise beyond her years. In the letter, she thanked me for my openness with the class and encouraged me to keep teaching. She assured me that time would take the pain away and to focus on the positive ways my mother impacted my life. Finally, she reminded me to take joy in those people that I still had. To me, this was a not-so-subtle reminder that you never know what others have gone through, regardless of their age.

I felt compelled to part with things. We sold our furniture and bought new. I gave a mountain of clothes to charity. Books, boxes of stuff, stupid unnecessary shit—gone. I started working on an old guitar. It was my first brand-new electric guitar—a Cort Explorer—purchased at a small music store in Ravenna that is long gone. I had added a Washburn Wonderbar tremolo system when I was in high school. Installing the locking nut required that I permanently remove the truss rod cover that displayed the Cort logo. I had my senior picture taken with this guitar. It had looked the same for years. This was not a guitar that I played. I stored it. I still had the original Cort logo truss rod cover among my copious collection of guitar parts. For some reason, I wanted to return the presence of the Cort truss rod cover on the headstock and in the process, broke a screw off in the wood and had to dig a ghastly hole to remove it. Not only that, but the neck was torqued, and the electronics were messed up. Was my wanting to restore it a vain and desperate attempt to symbolically restore the past? Probably. Fuck it. I sold it. I had been doing nothing but dragging it around from place to place anyway. It wasn't really playable. Just a piece of the past. So I started thinning the herd.

My grandpa Pishney's half brother had given me a 1965 Teisco bass guitar and an old Lectrolab tube amp when I was about sixteen. I never really played it; I just kept it. It was a cool guitar and a good vintage tube amp, but I decided to part with them both and posted them on Craigslist. The amp sold right away, and the guy buying it assured me that it would be well used in the studio. I didn't really give a shit what he did with it. The bass guitar took a little longer, but I did get a call. Two guys showed up to take a look at it. These were a couple of older guys. Older than me, for sure, and one just looked different. He dressed a little too young for his age, but he pulled it off. He looked like "someone." Ya know what I mean? The potential buyer said he wanted it because he had one just like it back in '65. He asked me if I had a group. I said I play around town a little. He followed that with, "yeah, me and Derek here, we used to play with Ted Nugent." I said, "oh, yeah?" Partially not believing and partially not caring about anyone who played with the right-wing, gun-totin' nut job. Regardless, some of those early songs were great guitar tunes, and it was then that I remembered that Nugent did not sing on those early songs. It struck me that they were legit. I looked at the other guy and said, "So you're the voice on Stranglehold?" He said, "not only that, I cowrote that song." Derek St. Holmes and Dave Kiswiney were standing in my living room buying a guitar from me. I fucking love this town.

I had been sleeping in the same bed that I had when I was a child. Yes, I was married, forty years old, and we slept in my childhood bed. The set was all full size, solid wood, and included two dressers. It was made in Amish country in southern Ohio and probably dated back to the 1940s. There was really nothing wrong with it, so I never thought about getting anything new. Right around this time, it started raining in Middle Tennessee. It kept raining steadily day and night. The first week of May was the great Nashville flood of 2010. They originally called it a one-hundred-year flood and later upgraded it to a five-hundred-year flood. No one had ever seen anything like it. The water covered speed limit signs. We watched a house floating down the swollen river. Whole communities were trapped because there was only one road into the development and that road was flooded. Poor reflection on the city planners. The Grand Ole Opry House stage was under water. The shores of the Cumberland covered lower Broadway and lapped beyond 2nd avenue. Many musicians lost priceless instruments.

In the aftermath, it was a regular occurrence to see piles of flood-damaged items amassed on the roadside for pickup. Driving home from the gym one morning, I noticed a giant headboard to a cherry sleigh bed at the end of someone's driveway. I abruptly stopped and asked about it. The homeowner was understandably disconnected. He said I could have it and he also had the other pieces but one of the side rails had a large piece of wood broken off it. I smiled inside thinking how the bed may have broken. With my years of wood working experience, I knew that I could fix it. Over the next several weeks, I spent countless hours on my back patio stripping, repairing, and refinishing the bed. It was incredibly therapeutic. Up to and during this time, I would randomly begin to sob involuntarily, like something that needed to get out. I remember more than once working on the bed when these feelings overtook me and I found myself with my head on my forearm, leaning against the wall as tears splashed on the aggregate patio floor in the Tennessee spring air. There was a song that had been on my mind, and I had been blatantly avoiding it. I knew I had to get it over with, so one day after working on the bed, I sat in my studio and with my back to the speakers, listened to "What Sarah Said" by Death Cab for Cutie.

I wept uncontrollably. To the point that my cheeks hurt, and I couldn't catch my breath. And then it was over. I stopped. I regained my breath and dried my swollen face. My being felt as though it had been exorcised. The bed was finished within the next few weeks. I bought a new mattress and box springs and sold my childhood bedroom suit to a couple who had lost their furniture in the flood.

The hospice program offers free grief counseling to family members. I decided to take advantage of it. This is when I met Allison, my therapist at the local hospice office in Franklin. I opened up to her about so many things that I had never told anyone, and it proved to be very healing and restorative. When I disclosed to her my struggle with extreme anxiety, she gave me a copy of *From Panic to Power* by Lucinda Bassett, which literally changed my life. In Buddhist and Stoic philosophies, it is understood that there are no good things or bad things. There are only things. Who knows what is good or bad? Fearing death and lamenting the inevitable is like the dog being pulled by a cart who whines and attempts to pull back. The dog is going where the cart is going no matter what, so by resisting, the dog is making itself unhappy and missing the present moment. I had a breakthrough with Allison regarding my anxiety and mild depression because of the grief counseling. I will always see this as a gift from my mother.

My mom wanted no funeral. Her wish was to be cremated and have her ashes buried on top of my grandmother's grave. I knew this because she made sure to tell us every time the topic came up or when she was moving to a new place where she would surely be leaving "feet first." I would ask, "How do we do that?" She would say, "Just get a bunch of beer and go down to the cemetery in the middle of the night and dig a hole." Yeah, I can see it now:

Officer: "What are you doing here?"

Me: "Oh, just digging a hole to bury my mom's ashes in my grandma's grave. Is there a problem?"

But we made it happen. Since my cousin Beth is a deputy sheriff, she knows the right people in that rural county to get things done. We planned the burial for Mother's Day, and we all gathered at Beth's house that evening for a cookout and drinks. The hole had been previously dug by a backhoe (not me with a shovel) and after dark, we all drove the mile or so to the cemetery. It was emotional and at the same time satisfying to me because she was getting what she wanted. She didn't get that much in life. We all arrived in the dark of the Ohio night. Aunt Marty asked if anyone wanted to say anything. I did. In so many words, I simply said that I did not know if I had the strength to go through what my mother did in her life and keep the positive attitude that she was known for. I shared a quote that I have always remembered by Edmund Burke: "The true way to mourn the dead is to take care of the living that belong to them." I thanked them all for taking care of me and expressed gratitude that this had brought us all together. I placed the box that contained my mother's ashes in the hole in the ground. It rested, touching the vault with my grandmother's casket. I broke the seal on a bottle of Jim Beam, took a generous swallow and poured a fair amount into the hole before passing the bottle around. It was over. Just like that. That's all there was. The Peggy Lee song, "Is That All There Is?" came back to me again. I never really understood why but I never forgot it. It's such a dark lyric conveying that nothing really matters. If that's all there is to life; inevitable death, then let's just have a good time.

As we drove out of the cemetery, on the same path where my mom's wheelchair lift had been stuck seventeen years before, my cousin Jill commented on the single star that glowed in the night sky. Without thinking I said, "That's actually a planet." She said, "I didn't know planets shined." I felt like a dick immediately. Still do. Sometimes it's better to say nothing at all.

So it was over. Her pain was over. My worry was over. Even though I don't believe in closure, there was a sense of the end of a chapter. She got her final wish of having her ashes buried with her mother in the middle of the night. And we had a bunch of beer.

Elizabeth Ann Pishney (McClain)
1948–2010

-12-
Why Not You?

During this initial writing, something happened that warranted this final chapter. Let's go back to 1996. Sometime during that year, I suddenly experienced numbness in my left hand that was progressively worse from my index finger to my pinky. My mother immediately feared that it was MS. It almost seemed like she wanted it to be an MS diagnosis. That thought never entered my mind. I had recently picked up a window air conditioning unit from the floor using my back and figured it was probably from that. I must have pinched a nerve or pulled something. But it was very difficult to play guitar. Of my many guitars, my main axe, is a 1981 Gibson Les Paul Custom, which weighs a little over ten pounds, and it can really take its toll on the shoulder and back, especially after a long gig. So, I bought a new, elastic guitar strap to relieve some of the weight that could be pinching a nerve in my shoulder. It was very challenging to play with the numbness, so I didn't play for a while because of the weird sensation. It felt like the end of something. The band was broken up, and I was not gigging much. I went to a reflexologist. At night, I would lie in bed with spring-loaded clothespins on my fingertips to stimulate the nerves. It seemed to help. I also had some numbness in my left leg, but no loss of mobility.

A new day in Franklin, TN. *Photo: Amelie Mendoza*

My family doc sent me to get an MRI of my spine and brain. I would be inside of the MRI machine for about an hour, and they gave me headphones to listen to the radio. I chose the now-defunct local alternative rock station, 107.9 WENZ The End in Cleveland. The hum and buzz of the machine created weird harmonic overtones in the music. Now, every time that I hear "Name" by the Goo Goo Dolls, I think of that damn machine. The tests showed nothing abnormal. I did learn, though, that I had spina bifida occulta. Very simply, this is an abnormality in one or more of the vertebrae. They told me it was nothing. I could have lived my whole life and never known. Gradually, the numbness went away and never returned.

Many years later after starting graduate school, I was diagnosed with panic/anxiety disorder. This had been going on for a very long time, and I had never realized it. It got increasingly worse as I progressed in higher education. It had always been present, but I didn't realize the shortness of breath, the paralyzed feelings, and the constant cloudy brain as a problem. The day that I almost drove myself to the hospital because I thought I was having a heart attack was when I decided to make an appointment with my family doctor and request a physical. He asked, "Why do you want a physical?" I told him my symptoms: I was frequently short of breath, dizzy, felt like I was "wrapped up" in something, my speech sometimes felt like it slurred, my heart raced. All of this went away at night or after I had a couple of drinks. He said bluntly, "You're having panic attacks," as he looked down, writing on his clip board. This guy was a doctor of osteopathic medicine and suggested yoga or meditation. I was already familiar with basic yoga practice, and I knew many different relaxation and meditation techniques after studying Tai Chi Chuan and delving into Buddhism for many years. He never mentioned medication. I probably would not have taken it anyway.

Looking back, I had been having anxiety issues for years. I used to throw up in the morning on my way to high school. When I was in my early twenties, I would drive several miles into the next town to wash my car because I did not want to be seen by anyone who knew me. I only went grocery shopping when I visited my mom in Kent for the same reason. It never prevented me from going on stage, but the time leading up to that was pure hell. I felt stuck to the ground. I was always outside of myself, and my life felt like a dream. The diagnosis made sense. When I talked to my father on the phone, my heart would race, I was short of breath, and eventually got a headache. But as grad school progressed, the symptoms worsened. Much of this anxiety, I am sure, had to do with the fact that my mother did not understand the concept or rigors of graduate studies (nor did I: I had no idea what the fuck I had gotten myself into), and she placed unrealistic expectations on me. She would call and want me to come over and do yard work while I was in the midst of writing exhaustive research papers, working in the geography department as per my graduate assistantship and researching for my thesis proposal. I get it. She was lonely. Or just trying to control me. I really think that she resented me. Either way, it was frustrating, and I hated it. And that energy had to manifest itself somewhere. I learned to deal with the anxiety and accept it as part of who I was. I could deal with it. It wasn't going to kill me. At least I didn't think so, even though it sometimes felt like it. It became an unwelcomed friend that I could always rely on to be there. Fucking bastard. Yoga, breathing exercises, meditation, working out, peppermint tea; these all helped with the symptoms. And Scotch whisky. That helped too.

I survived grad school. I survived my first adjunct teaching gigs. After several years as a part-time instructor in Ohio and Tennessee, I got a full-time temporary position at Middle Tennessee State University the year after my mom died. In addition, I had a dual service agreement with Motlow State Community College where I was responsible for two online classes. That's when the anxiety attacks started to get the best of me. I would find that at the end of my classes, I was so wound up that my body actually hurt. I hobbled my way back to my office at the end of the long hallway and collapsed in the chair behind my desk. My contract at MTSU was for fifteen credit hours per semester and I taught three classes in a row, back-to-back on certain days. After class, it was hard to breathe, my head felt like it was in a vice, and I could not wait to get off my feet. I would sit in my office for at least an hour or two before I went home. Though it would still be a couple years before I sought help.

After my mom died, the sessions with Allison at hospice were invaluable to me regarding the anxiety disorder. The copy of *From Panic to Power*, yoga, and meditation were game changers. I had learned how to deal with so much of this mess that it seemed normal and the way that I was supposed to be. But I was also aware that I was not/could not do many of the things that I used to do. Things that I loved. I had basically forgotten about playing live because it was too hard. Something that I lived to do had just become part of the past, almost like it never happened. And one day, my brain just flipped. I was tired. Tired of feeling trapped and exhausted. Tired of feeling lost and foggy. Tired of living this way. Just tired. I had only occasionally thought about it, but I finally made an appointment with my doctor to discuss my anxiety and possibly get on some medication. I exhaled and made the call with a feeling of weary surrender. I scheduled the appointment and surprisingly, showed up. I spoke with the nurse before the doctor came in and I answered a questionnaire. I don't remember the questions, but I answered "yes" to damn near all of them. She and I talked. I was holding back tears as I described my symptoms, and she outwardly empathized with her eyes. Then the doctor came in. She and I conversed, reviewed the questionnaire, and discussed my symptoms. I told her that I felt like I was giving up. She said, "You're not giving up, you're taking control." She wrote me a script of a starter dose (25mg) of Sertraline, commercially known as Zoloft. I asked about alcohol. She told me it was ok, just space it out. I took that as maybe I shouldn't wash the pill down with a Martini. Nevertheless, I didn't drink when I first started the meds. With trepidation, I took the first pill in the evening and went to bed.

During the same time that I saw my doc for the anxiety, coincidentally, I discovered something. For quite a few years, I had been aware that if I did not work out regularly, I got weak and didn't feel quite right. The harder I worked out, the better I felt. Seems obvious, but there was something else. I was never a runner, but it felt like it was more difficult than ever to run and even walking a long distance tired me out. I was often dizzy, and it was especially hard to walk down steps. Then one day, I did something to my knee. I don't know what I did, but it hurt. I started wearing a knee brace and found that I walked better and felt stronger. I didn't feel as clumsy and felt more grounded overall. I thought that there must be something wrong with my knee. So, I made an appointment with an orthopedic doctor. He did tests, took X-rays, and watched me walk. With a concerned look on his face he said, "There's nothing wrong with your knees." Because I was experiencing foot drop and had an odd gait, he suggested that I see someone in neurology.

The neurologist looked considerably younger than me and at first, it was hard for me to take him seriously. In my mind, he was Doogie Houser, MD. But he went to Ohio State, so that made him okay. We talked about music; we talked about bourbon; we talked a lot. He ordered a laundry list of tests. I went to the blood lab with my orders, and they took nine vials. Nine. I left the lab and could not stop shivering due to the blood loss. I guess that is better than my usual drifting off into limbo from low blood sugar. The blood labs showed nothing unusual, and I could not believe that my liver profile was as good as the numbers reported. He knew of my mother's condition and even though it is not necessarily hereditary, he wanted to rule out multiple sclerosis. He ordered an MRI of the brain with and without contrast. I spent about forty-five minutes in the tube listening to the buzzing and rhythmic banging of the magnetic machine (much like I did back in 1996 except this time, I had no headphones and music). I survived the tube, and upon emerging, the technician asked me, "So why is he testing you for MS?" I'm sure he was not supposed to have this conversation with me, but I indulged. I told him that he wants to rule it out and the tech said, "MS usually appears as lesions." I took it as that the image did not show anything significant and left feeling nothing. This was just another step. I didn't have MS.

A week or so went by and I got a call to come in for the MRI results. We looked at the images in a darkened room. Of course, I was anxious. Any time that you get to see your internals, it's bound to be a little awkward. But they showed relatively nothing. Except one spot. One very small spot on the right side of my brain. A spot so small that he had to zoom in to show it to me. He said, "It could be nothing. It could be an error on the scan." But there was only one way to find out. Lumbar puncture. Spinal tap. I said, "What would *you* do?" He said, "I would do it, just to rule it out. But I will be very surprised if this is MS." I scheduled the lumbar puncture.

He told me what the procedure was like, and I also made the mistake of reading about it. I took half of a Hydrocodone before my appointment just to chill a bit. They called my name, and I went back to the room. I lay on the table on my side, and he numbed me with Lidocaine. He then stuck the needle into my lumbar to bleed the spinal fluid. I felt it. Not pain, but something weird. He shot me up with more Lidocaine and tried again. And again. He couldn't get between my vertebrae because they were too tight. I began to feel dreamy and not because of the Hydro-codone. I think I was about to pass out. I asked the nurse to rub my feet. That made me feel better. He asked that I sit upright on the table so he could get a better angle and hit my spinal column. Once. Twice. He said, "Got it." And it was over. I felt nauseated, disoriented, and drained. I was told to go home, sit upright in bed, drink a Coke, and expect a headache. That all happened. He would call with the results.

A few days went by. I had started the Sertraline about four days earlier and could tell the difference in the way that I felt. I had somewhat of a headache on the first day, but after that it was gone. I did not feel medicated, I just felt...normal. Normal like I had not felt in many, many years. I walked around my apartment complex parking lot without feeling dizzy or disoriented. I was stable. My head was clear, and I strolled around with new eyes (or old eyes from before my anxiety disorder). Either way, everything looked different, and I felt normal. It was weird. Like I was back from a long trip, and no one knew I was gone. Not even me. The more time passed, I felt as though all my problems were anxiety related and this little green pill, this beautiful tiny pill, had fixed everything.

When I was a kid, we used to attend the annual Christmas party at the Paris township community center not far from our house. Every child brought a new, wrapped toy for the gift exchange and at the end of the event, each kid got to pick a gift from the large box full of wrapped presents. Some gifts were small, square boxes that could be anything. Others were obvious, like a coloring book and crayons, wrapped so that the box of Crayolas was clearly apparent on the edge of the flat package. No attempt was made to conceal the shape of the contents with the festive paper. I must have been disappointed by this gift in the past because I wanted nothing less than a coloring book and crayons for Christmas. The year that is most vivid in my memory is the one in which I picked that very package in hopes that somehow, someway, this obvious awkwardly shaped package was not pages of black and white outlines of Mickey Mouse or Scooby Doo with a container of colored wax designed to make my developing mind believe that I was an actual artist. No. It had to be something else. Something fascinating and cool. But what, I had no idea. I couldn't resist the temptation. I chose the deformed package and as I looked up at my mother with a smile I said, "I hope it's not a coloring book and crayons." She gave a look that I cannot describe. Something like, "Really, how dumb is this kid?" Or maybe if you're from the South, "Bless his heart." As I tore away the paper, the mystery was revealed. It was a coloring book and crayons. I cried. She hurried me over to the box while no one was looking. There were only a few small gifts remaining at the bottom of the cardboard box, one being the Matchbox car that I had chosen to bring. I picked it up, unwrapped it to no surprise, and we went home.

I was alone in our apartment when the doctor called. I don't remember his exact words. I don't even remember saying "hello." I only remember seeing his face in my mind's eye and hearing his voice in both of my ears when he said slowly, with disappointment, "It's MS." He sounded defeated. A strange heat spread across my shoulder blades that I had never felt before and haven't since. I wasn't sad. I wasn't angry and I wasn't scared. I wasn't anything, except that little kid at the community center who was hoping for something completely different when he knew goddamn well what the truth was. The doctor was somber, most likely because he had been so sure that this was not multiple sclerosis. I told him that many of my symptoms had lessened since I had been on the Sertraline, as if his diagnosis was a mistake. He said he wasn't surprised. I asked how certain he was of the diagnosis. He was certain. Nevertheless, he assured me that I would be fine and told me that he would treat me like family. I was seemingly unfazed by the news. After all, I had a gig coming up and had rehearsal in a couple of hours.

The diagnosis made a lot of sense. The fatigue after cycling, teaching, or just bringing in the groceries, the clumsiness walking, the stiffness; it was all part of it. Goddamn it, anyhow. I can't get away from it—MS has always been present in my life, and now it always would be.

Honestly, when the diagnosis came, one of my first thoughts was, "Well, I've got a hell of an ending for my book."

He started me on the DMT (disease modifying therapy) Copaxone, the same drug my mom had been on for a while, but she was too far advanced for it to have much, if any, benefit. Copaxone is designed to give the immune system something to attack other than itself and prevent the disease from progressing. Three injections a week. A nurse came to my apartment and trained me on doing the injections with a device called AutoJect that came with the first prescription of preloaded syringes. You load the syringe in the device, chose your injection site, pinch some fat, place the tip on your skin, and squeeze the button. With a loud "click," the device rapidly propels the solution into your subcutaneous fat. More often than not, there is a lump or a bubble at the injection site that could last for a couple days. I think that generally, the AutoJect is designed for those with needle phobias or a lack of dexterity in their fingers. It is an effective, but clumsy device and much of the site reaction is due to the speed of the injection. After only a couple of weeks, I called the nurse and asked to be trained on manual injections.

In addition to the drug therapy, I started physical therapy, which was a game changer for me. In just two months with the combination of the DMT and the physical therapy, many of my symptoms lessened, and I felt stronger. The drug reps and nurses frequently called to ask about my condition. I told them that some of my symptoms were lessening. They reminded me that "Copaxone does not treat symptoms," which I am sure they are required to say. Nevertheless, my nurse agreed that the chemistry of the brain is changed by the drug therapy, and it makes sense that symptoms would be affected. Doesn't matter. I felt better. I felt like I was in control.

This was all big news for me, the diagnosis, the therapy, and the one person in my life that would understand the most, was gone. I am grateful, however, that the experience of my mother's MS journey lessened my anxiety. I am well aware of the uncertainty and fear suffered by the newly diagnosed, but I had experienced MS my whole life as an observer and a caregiver. My mom was diagnosed in her twenties when there was little to no treatment. I was forty-five, and medicine had progressed exponentially. I was not worried. I was actually a little relieved. It wasn't cancer; it wasn't ALS or a brain tumor. If my symptoms stabilized and never progressed, I could deal with it. Over the next couple of years, I maintained my physical therapy exercises and altered my diet significantly. I was always active and ate well, but now I had a greater purpose. I still get tired easily doing simple tasks but with a little scheduled rest, I am fine. My brain scan has not changed since the first one—no new or active lesions. As I have heard many speakers and nurses say regarding the new therapies, "This ain't your momma's MS anymore." For me, that phrase is quite literal. Do I wish that I didn't have it? What kind of an idiot would not? But this disease has given me something to overcome, something to rise above.

At this point, you might be expecting me to describe how my diagnosis and the pending uncertain future has led me to some spiritual awakening and how I am now following a path of righteousness and clean living, seeking to convert all readers to my way of thinking and being. Nope. I am still not religious, and I have at least a couple glasses of wine damn near every day. But that's ok. And what you do is ok, too. As Fonzie once said, "Live and let live. Can you dig it?" You do you. It works for me, but some days are better than others, that's just the way it is with anything. I don't think what I do will work for everyone. Your MS ain't my MS. Everybody's path is different. Your journey is your own.

But I do feel like I have an unfair advantage dealing with this. And with that knowledge, I feel as if it is my calling to share my path with others on both sides, as a caregiver and a patient. It's hard for me to play shows but I still do it, though infrequently. I can tell the difference in the way I feel when I don't take care of myself with bad food and too many cocktails. My neurologist says, "I don't feel good when I don't take care of myself, either." Touché. Honestly, I don't think about it much. I am lucky. It does not impact my daily life significantly, and there is very little that I do not do because of it. It does not define me. As the saying goes, I have MS, but it does not have me. Yeah, it's cliché, but it's true.

Up until this point, I have rarely told anyone, other than a few close friends, because I know that people treat you differently when they think something is wrong with you. And the fewer people who know, the less likely it is that they will spread false information.

It's almost as if a new life started after my diagnosis and treatment. I definitely feel better, both physically and mentally. My wife loves me. I know this because of all of the boring gigs she's sat through over the years. She knows when I need to rest, and she knows how to take care of me so that I stay healthy. I have a great support group of fellow MS friends in the Nashville area, and we meet socially, oftentimes celebrating our successes and sharing positive info over lunch. All of the past is gone, and our future is unwritten. Dwelling on what once was or worrying about what is to come is a waste of energy. All we have is now, for better or worse. All things considered, I have it pretty damn good, and everything in my past has led up to the person that I am today.

And I wouldn't change a thing.

Steve McClain is a singer/songwriter and guitarist based in Nashville, TN. He was born and raised in Northeast Ohio and earned a BA and MA in geography at Kent State University. He teaches geography and earth science at Columbia State and Nashville State Community Colleges and music at Franklin Brentwood Arts Academy in Middle Tennessee. www.stevemcclain.com